Series Editor Dale Gunthorp
Editor Lesley Firth
Design Peter Benoist
Picture Research Maggie Colbeck
Production Philip Hughes
Illustrations Ron Hayward Associates
John Shackell
Marilyn Day
Tony Payne
Maps Matthews and Taylor Associates
Consultant Ursula Sharma

Photographic sources Key to positions
of illustrations: *(T)* top, *(C)* centre, *(B)*
bottom, *(L)* left, *(R)* right.
Air India and Government of India Tourist
Office *9(BL)*, *11(TL)*, *22(TL)*, *22(BL)*,
23(T), *23(B)*, *27(TL)*, *27(TR)*, *33(TR)*,
35(TR), *42(BL)*, *43(BL)*, *45(TR)*.
Camera & Pen *15(TR)*, *24-5(B)*, *41(BR)*,
44(B), *49(BR)*, *53(B)*. Tony Duffy
51(BL). Patrick Eagar *45(TL)*.
Mark Edwards *11(TR)*, *18(BL)*,
18(BR), *19(BR)*, *22(BR)*, *24(TL)*,
31(TL), *31(BL)*, *32(BR)*, *33(TL)*,
34(T), *35(TL)*, *39(TL)*, *43(TL)*,
45(BL), *47(TR)*, *48(T)*, *48(C)*, *50(BR)*,
53(TR). Mary Evans Picture Library
36(BL), *38(B)*. Government of India
41(TR). Richard and Sally Greenhill
12(B), *30(T)*, *39(BL)*. Sonia Halliday
Photographs (Photo: Peter Marsden) *2-3*,
26(TL), *50(TL)*. Tom Hanley *21(BL)*,
29(BR), *41(BL)*, *46(T)*. Robert
Harding Associates *8(B)*. Nick Hedges
51(TR). IBH Publishing Co. *29(BL)*.
Victor Kennett *9(CR)*, *19(TL)*,
25(CR), *43(TR)*, *43(CR)*, *47(BL)*,
47(BR). William MacQuitty *32(TL)*.
Margaret Murray *14(T)*, *15(BL)*, *17(T)*,
20(BL), *20(BR)*, *24(BL)*, *27(BL)*,
32(BL), *34(B)*, *46(B)*, *47(TL)*, *48(B)*,
49(BL), *52(CR)*, *53(TL)*. Mansell
Collection *38(TR)*. Bury Peerless
25(BR). Pictor *6-7*, *11(BR)*, *11(BL)*,
12(T), *13(B)*, *18(T)*, *19(TR)*, *20(TL)*,
27(BR), *35(BR)*, *52(B)*. Productions
Television Rencontre *28(T)*, *38(TL)*,
40(TL), *42(R)*. Radio Times Hulton
Picture Library *39(TR)*, *40(B)*,
40-41(T). Servizio Editoriale
Fotografico *9(TR)*, *26(B)*, *34(C)*,
37(BR), *49(CL)*, *52(T)*. Spectrum
50(TL). Victoria and Albert Museum
36(BR), *37(TR)*, *37(BL)*. ZEFA *35(BR)*.

First published 1975
Reprinted 1976, 1978, 1980, 1982, 1984

Macdonald & Co (Publishers) Ltd
Maxwell House, Worship Street,
London EC2A 2EN
Member of BPCC plc

© Macdonald Educational Ltd. 1975

ISBN 0 356 05102 1 (cased edition)
ISBN 0 356 06522 7 (limp edition)

Made and printed by
Purnell & Sons (Book Production) Ltd
Paulton, England
Member of BPCC plc

Colour reproduction by
Fotomecanica Iberico, Madrid

India

the land and its people

Natasha Talyarkhan

Macdonald Educational

Contents

Early India

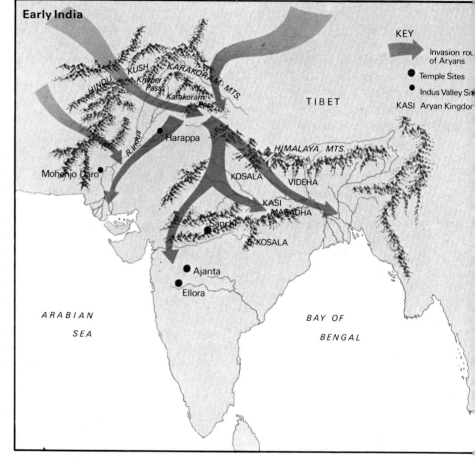

Early India

KEY

→ Invasion rou of Aryans
● Temple Sites
● Indus Valley Si
KASI Aryan Kingdor

An ancient civilization

Indian history began about 5,000 years ago in the Indus valley. The people who lived there built fine cities at Mohenjo Daro and Harappa and probably traded with Mesopotamia and Sumeria. Seals, ornaments and other objects have been dug up which show that they wove cotton clothes, had their own handwriting and may have worshipped the bull. Historians say these people are the ancestors of the Dravidians who now live in South India.

The original Hindus were Aryan invaders from the north. The Aryans used iron, loved adventure and raced horse-drawn chariots. They collected the Hindu holy books and developed a rigid social system. Society was divided into groups or castes who had fixed jobs and could not intermarry.

Emperors of India

In 326 B.C. Alexander the Great, tempted by tales of India's wealth, invaded India. He left Greek generals to look after his territories. Chandragupta Maurya, the first great emperor of India, overthrew the Greek garrisons and founded the Mauryan dynasty. He built up a huge empire stretching across North India. His adviser Kautilya helped him organize a terrifying spy system and then wrote a book about the arts of government called the *Arthashastra*.

Mauryan power faded and was replaced in the fourth century A.D. by the Guptas. These Hindu kings were kind and just and under their rule the arts blossomed. Further south, a succession of dynasties ruled over areas stretching from the Arabian Sea to the Bay of Bengal.

South India had its own rulers. These kings traded in spices with the Middle East and the Far East, built sophisticated irrigation works and beautiful temples.

From the eighth century onward, India was invaded by Muslim Arabs and Turks filled with religious fervour against Hindu "idolaters". By the twelfth century they had conquered northern India. They ruled India until the time of the Moghul invasions.

▲ The Aryans were semi-barbaric tribes who invaded India in c. 1500 B.C. They pushed the Indus peoples into South India and set up their own kingdoms on the banks of the Ganges and Jumna. They were not a peaceful people and fought many wars.

▼ Mohenjo Daro, now in Pakistan, was a river port of the Indus valley civilization. The Indus peoples planned their cities well. They built straight roads intersecting at right angles, laid drains and lived in two-storey brick houses with bathrooms.

▲ The Great Stupa at Sanchi, seen through the northern gateway. This hemispherical burial mound was built during Ashoka's reign and contains Buddhist relics. The four gateways, added later, are elaborately carved with scenes from Buddha's life.

◄ Four scowling lions cap Ashoka's column at Sarnath. Ashoka, Chandragupta Maurya's grandson, had similar pillars inscribed with Buddhist teachings erected all over India. He became a Buddhist when he saw the misery caused by war. The Indian government has adopted the lions for its official seal.

▲ This fresco of Buddha is one of the many paintings which adorn the Ajanta cave temples. Other paintings show Buddhist life 1,600 years ago and narrate ancient Buddhist stories. Ajanta was chosen by Buddhist monks as a site for a monastery. They carved 29 cave temples and sanctuaries out of the sheer rock face and decorated them with frescoes and religious sculpture.

◄ The Ellora cave temples were built by Buddhists, Jains and Hindus. From the seventh century A.D. Buddhist monks began carving temples into the hillside. Some years later Hindu and Jain monks added their own temples. One of the most beautiful temples, Kailasanath, was built by the Rashtrakutas, Hindu rulers of the Deccan. It represents Mount Kailash, the god Shiva's snowy abode in the Himalayas.

A continent of a country

The face of the land

India, the seventh largest country in the world, is a land of striking contrasts. It has mountains and plains, deserts and swamps, sandy beaches and dense forests.

In the north is the great wall of the Himalayas which cuts India off from central Asia. Some of the highest mountains in the world are in this range. The word Himalaya means "abode of snow" in Sanskrit.

South of the Himalayas is the hot fertile Indo-Gangetic plain. It is so flat that between Delhi and Calcutta it only varies in height by 200 metres (656 feet). The sacred river Ganges flows past towns and villages to reach the Bay of Bengal. Over one third of India's population lives in this area.

The triangular part of India south of the Vindhya mountains is called the Deccan. This plateau is guarded from the seas by two densely-forested mountain ranges known as the Eastern and Western Ghats.

Along India's long coastline are some of the most beautiful, palm-fringed sandy beaches in the world.

India's agriculture is very dependent on the monsoon rains. Unfortunately, they are unreliable. One year they may cause floods and the next year the farmers may be faced with drought.

The faces of the people

India, with 638 million people, has the second largest population in the world. Its people are a mixture of four racial types: Caucasian, Dravidian, Mongoloid and Aboriginal.

The people of the Indo-Gangetic plain are Caucasians. The Sikhs, who come from the Punjab, are tall and fair-skinned.

Quite different are the short flat-nosed and darker-skinned Tamils of South India. They are Dravidians and speak Tamil, an ancient Dravidian language.

The Assamese, with their flat noses and slant eyes, belong to the Mongoloid race.

India's aborigines, such as the Santals and the Mundas, live in the jungles and hills of central and East India.

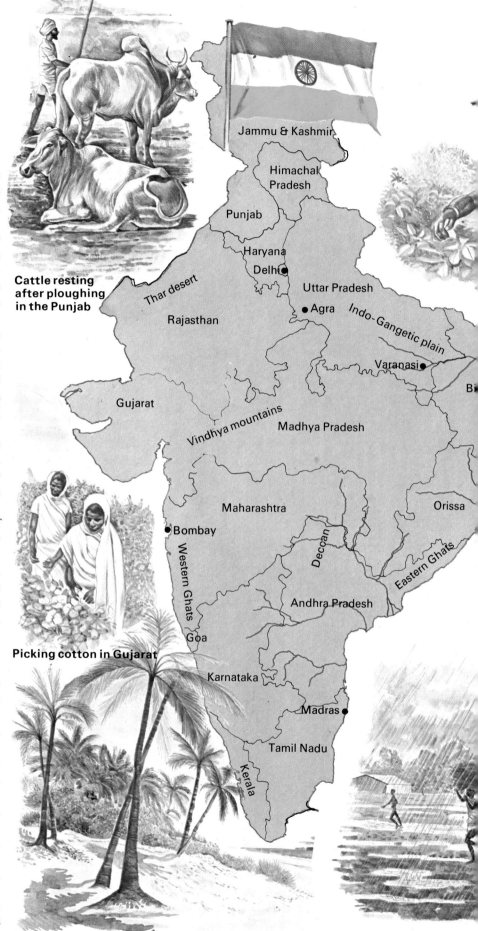

Cattle resting after ploughing in the Punjab

Picking cotton in Gujarat

Palm-fringed beach in Goa

The monsoon

Picking tea in Assam

Arunachal Pradesh

Bhutan

Assam

Nagaland

Meghalaya

Manipur

Tripura

Mizoram

st
...gal

Calcutta

▲ The beautiful valleys of Kashmir provide rich pasture for cattle. In the distance are the snow-capped Himalayas. During the winter the Kashmiris carry a little stove inside their cloaks to keep warm. The *kangri*, as it is called, is held in a basket hung from their necks by a long strap.

...Soldiers riding camels in the Thar desert ...Rajasthan, where the camel is the chief ...eans of transport. The desert sands are ...h in minerals, but grow little apart ...m thorny shrubs. The longest canal in ...e world is being built to bring water ...m the Punjab to this dry area.

▲ Tall office blocks in Bombay, the capital of Maharashtra. Bombay is built on an island and has a magnificent natural harbour. It is one of Asia's largest seaports and is an important industrial and commercial centre. The population of Bombay is about six million.

▲ This man is gathering coconuts in Kerala. When he gets to the top of the palm tree he will hack off the coconuts and let them fall to the sandy ground. Bystanders beware! Kerala is India's main producer of coir matting which is made from the dried husk of the coconut.

11

A cradle of many faiths

► Farmers praying at the Jumma Masjid, a mosque in Delhi. Devout Muslims must pray five times a day facing Mecca, give alms, fast for one month in a year and make a pilgrimage to Mecca once in their lives. Muslims believe in one God. The Koran, as revealed to the prophet Mohammed, is their holy book. India has the third largest population of Muslims in the world.

▼ Hindus believe that bathing in the River Ganges will wash away all their sins. Every Spring thousands of Hindus pour into Varanasi during the festival of Magh Mela. They visit the temples to lay offerings before the gods and to take a dip in the holy waters. It is every Hindu's dearest wish to visit Varanasi once in his life and if possible, to die there.

The religion of the Hindus

Over the centuries India has absorbed all the major religions of the world. It has Hindus, Muslims, Buddhists, Jains, Sikhs, Christians, Parsees and Jews.

Hinduism and Islam are the main Indian religions. The religion of the Hindus comes from the ancient Aryans who sang beautiful hymns to various gods. These were later collected as the four Vedas—the sacred texts of the Hindus. Over the 1,000 years before they were written down, one can see the development towards belief in one god. The many gods in the Hindu religion are really different aspects of this Divine Being. For example, Brahma represents the Creator, Vishnu the Preserver, and Shiva the Destroyer.

Hindus believe that the soul is eternal. It is born again and again in many different bodies until it finally becomes perfect. Karma, the actions in a previous life, determine a Hindu's position or caste in this life. Moksha is the state of perfection when the soul is freed from the cycle of life and death. It is achieved by meditation and abiding by one's *Dharma* or religious duty.

Two great prophets

Buddha was born a Hindu prince in 563 B.C. As a young man, Prince Siddhartha as he was then called, left his family and palace to search for the truth about life.

After years of penance and prayer he found the answer while meditating under a tree. He said that a person could not achieve *Nirvana*, or supreme happiness, if he was too attached to worldly pleasures or solely interested in mortifying the flesh. The only way to escape rebirth was to follow a Middle Path. Siddhartha was renamed Buddha (one who has knowledge) and preached a simple religion without ritual or caste.

Like Buddha, Guru Nanak disliked the rituals and caste system of the Hindus. He also disapproved of the hypocrisy of the Muslim priests of his time. His teachings were a blend of the good things in Islam and Hinduism. By the time he died in 1538, he had many followers known as Sikhs.

A Jain monk praying before a statue of Mahavira, the founder of Jainism. Jains believe in non-violence and that everything has a soul. They wear masks around their mouths to prevent small insects from dying when they breathe in.

Some minority religions

▲ Sikhs believe in one god. Most Sikhs wear the five Ks: *Kes* (long hair), *Kangha* (comb), *Kirpan* (sword), *Kara* (steel bangle) and *Kaccha* (short pants).

▲ Buddhists come from all over the world to pray at Bodhgaya, the place where Buddha received enlightenment. They follow the Eight-fold path preached by Buddha.

▲ A devotee meditating before Kali, the black goddess of Destruction, who wears a necklace of skulls. Followers of hers, the Thugs, used to make human sacrifices to her. Now she receives sweets, flowers and goats.

▲ Indian Christians may be Catholic or Protestant. Others may belong to the Syrian Orthodox Church. This was founded in 52 A.D. by St. Thomas, one of the twelve disciples, who is said to be buried in Madras.

The Indian way of life

▲ Religion plays a large part in Indian life. Many young men give up worldly life to become wandering holy men. They live on gifts of food and money, and sleep in temples or by wayside shrines. Holy men who worship the god Shiva carry a three-pronged stick.

▼ "All people are born unequal"

Hindu society has a built-in class-structure called the caste system. A person's status, job and future marriage are all defined by the caste into which he is born. Since his actions in his last life determine his caste in this one, he is not expected to complain.

A passage in the Vedas describes the origin of the four main castes. From the mouth of the god Brahma were born the Brahmins (priests); from his arms, the Kshatriyas (warriors and kings); from his thighs, the Vaishyas (merchants and landowners); and from his feet the Shudras (labourers). Outside this system were the untouchables or Chandalas. These were only allowed to do lowly jobs such as sweeping the streets.

In Aryan times, people could change their caste and do other jobs, but over the years the system became very rigid. People could only marry within their caste and do caste jobs. Today there are thousands of castes. The practice of untouchability, though forbidden by law, still exists.

Hospitality

Indians are renowned for their hospitali[ty] A visitor to an Indian home is norma[lly] invited to stay to dinner. After he has ea[ten] fit to burst, his hostess will say "But y[ou] haven't eaten anything". If he has co[me] from another town, he will be asked to st[ay] the night. A special mattress will be [un]rolled on the floor if there is no spare be[d.] Most visitors can stay for as long as they li[ke] and periods of six months are not unknow[n]. This is one of the reasons that Indian hot[els] do such poor business with their ow[n] countrymen.

Red tape

If one walks into any government office, o[ne] can hear people complaining about t[he] *babu* mentality of the Indians. A *babu* is [an] officious clerk. Long queues and for[m-]filling have become a part of Indian life. [A] person who gets to the front of a queue [is] bound to be sent back to fill in anoth[er] form, or because he has not had it stamp[ed] by the right official.

Rich people sometimes give large bri[bes] to officials, who then make sure that thin[gs] get done more quickly. Successive gover[n-]ments have promised action to try a[nd] eliminate this sort of corruption.

Vaishya

Kshatriya

Brahmin

Shudra

Untouchable

A woman with palms joined in the [tra]ditional greeting called *namaste* or [na]*maskar*. Indians greet each other in [dif]ferent ways depending on their [rel]ationship to the other person. Friends [wil]l embrace or shake hands and a young [pe]rson will bow down to touch his father's [fe]et as a sign of respect.

▼ In the crowded cities, people have to learn to live right on top of each other. Children play hide-and-seek inside the house, and everyone yells loudly to friends across the street. Meditation can help to achieve peaceful state of mind. To outsiders, Indians can seem very inquisitive and interfering. A stranger in India may be asked 'Where do you work?' and if single 'Why aren't you married?'

▲ Women meeting around the communal village well. Traditionally, Indian women have been subservient to men and have stuck to the company of other women. But they are now equal in law, and are beginning to exercise their rights.

▼ Job-hunters, students or even politicians consult a palmist or astrologer when in doubt. The astrologer comes into his own before a marriage when he has to compare the future couple's birth charts. If their stars are not in harmony, sometimes the marriage does not take place.

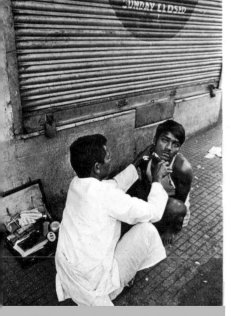

A young man being shaved by a barber in [a B]ombay street. Indians in the city are [ver]y fashion conscious, and imitate their [fav]ourite film stars. They copy their hair [sty]les, mannerisms and clothes. [We]sternized Indians pride themselves on [the]ir ability to keep up with the latest [styl]es from Europe. Perfumes, cosmetics, [wa]tches and clothes bought on trips abroad [are] highly prized.

The family commune

The joint family

Indian families are large, quarrelsome and very loving. They are held together by a strong sense of duty towards each other. Grandparents, uncles, aunts, children and various pets live crowded together under the same roof. This commune-like system is called a joint family. It used to be very widespread but is now less common in the cities.

The village day

The head of the family is usually the father or the eldest son. He has great power since he is in charge of all the money earned by the family. The mother-in-law too can be a bit of a dictator. She runs the communal kitchen and can be very unpleasant if her daughters-in-law do not obey her.

Children and old people benefit most from this system. If a child's father dies, or is away in the city, he and his mother are looked after by the rest of the family. Children have so many cousins to play with that they are seldom lonely. There are often noisy cricket and football matches between neighbouring families.

Parents, too, can be sure that they will be cared for in old age and remain an important part of the family. They look forward to the day when all they have to do is to look after their grandchildren.

How the family is changing

The joint family dates back over 4 years and is closely linked to the c system. It belongs to the days when a had to take up his father's trade.

Nowadays, young people have gre choice and take other jobs, often in the They live where their work takes them spend their salaries as they please.

In modern families, parents, children grandparents live together. There is n privacy. Women have greater freedom more of them go to work. Children l more chances to go to school and univer

The village home is not forgotten those who move to the cities. The fa always sends some money to the people remain behind in the village. There noisy family reunions for holidays special occasions like marriage.

▲ Gopal and his family live in a typical Indian village. The whole family rises before dawn so that Gopal can get to the fields before the sun gets too hot. He has a quick bath, gulps down his tea and rushes off to the fields. The children take their time milking the cow.

▲ Ramu and Lakshmi set out for school which is in the next village. On the way they meet their friends and get up to all kinds of mischief. Kamala, their mother, now has time to wash the dirty dishes.
When she has finished, she goes to the fields to help her husband.

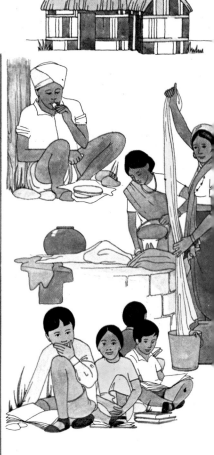

▲ The sun is beating down on Gopal's hea He decides to have his lunch and take a short nap. Kamala is washing clothes at th well. She gossips with her friends about li in the village. The children are still hard at work at school and longing for their lun break.

16

A typical family having lunch in a one-roomed flat in Bombay. The husband may work in a local government office and earn 300 rupees per month (£15). On this salary he looks after his family, pays the rent and sends money to his ageing parents in the village.

The wife is very house-proud. She cooks in one area of the room and gets very angry with the children if they dirty it. At night the family sleep on mattresses on the floor. In the morning the wife rolls them up and puts them back in the cupboard.

The children go to school locally and play in the streets. They miss the wide open spaces of the village.

The whole family looks forward to the weekend when they go to the cinema. The wife wears her best sari and decorates her hair with flowers her husband has bought for her. The children are very excited and hope their father will buy them an ice cream on their way to the cinema.

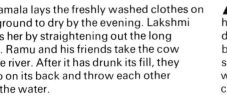

Kamala lays the freshly washed clothes on the ground to dry by the evening. Lakshmi helps her by straightening out the long ... Ramu and his friends take the cow the river. After it has drunk its fill, they jump on its back and throw each other to the water.

▲ Gopal and his friends can relax after their hard day's work. They sit in the twilight discussing local politics. The jokes get better and the laughter louder as the sun sets. The children are doing their homework, while Kamala cooks the dinner, a vegetable curry and *chapattis*.

▲ After their evening meal, the children go to sleep. Kamala waits until Gopal has had his fill before she eats. Before they go to bed, Gopal and Kamala take a short walk together in the cool night air. The village is quiet except for the soft chirruping of insects.

17

Custom and ceremony

Marriage

You can always tell when a wedding is taking place in India. The music from the bride's house can be heard from far away, and the house itself is decorated with flowers and coloured lights.

The best cooks are brought in to prepare the wedding food. Dozens of relatives rush around trying to help. The bride must be dressed in a red sari, her hands and feet painted with henna and her hair decorated with flowers and jewellery.

The wedding ceremony is held at an auspicious time selected by the astrologer. The bridegroom arrives on a horse accompanied by a loud band of musicians and men carrying lanterns.

After the wedding the wife puts red powder in her hair parting to show she is married. She must always wear bangles and coloured saris. When the husband dies, his widow smashes her bangles and dresses in white.

Most marriages are still arranged. When a child is grown up, the father will consult his family and friends to find a suitable partner. He may even advertise in the marriage columns of the newspapers.

Marriage discussions are held between the parents of the future couple. They often compare horoscopes to ensure that their children's stars are in harmony.

The boy and girl are lucky if they meet more than twice, and then they are strictly chaperoned by their families. Even though this system allows little freedom, it seems to work. The divorce rate in India is very low.

Superstitions

In India nearly everyone is superstitious. People dread the evil eye and mothers protect their children from it with charms and amulets. It is dangerous to praise a pretty girl, and you can upset a family by discussing its good fortune in case it brings on the evil eye.

Black magic is widespread. Priests do good business casting spells to ward off other priests' magic.

▼ A man laying offerings before two brightly painted, terracotta horses. The horses are set up by villagers as a thanks-offering for having been cured or rescued by the gods. They represent the speed with which the gods can reach people. Usually the statue of a god accompanies the horses. The god is placed with one foot over the neck of the demon from which the villager has been rescued. The villagers make the horses themselves and paint them in vivid colours. Each horse is replaced if it is damaged. This is a South Indian custom.

▲ The *mundan* or head-shaving ceremony. When a child is about a year old, a priest and a barber are called to the house. Prayers are said while the child's hair is shaved from his head. After the ceremony the parents distribute sweets to their family and friends. The ceremony is considered very important. It is one of the eight ceremonies a Hindu child may go through between birth and marriage. Other important ceremonies are the name-giving and the sacred thread ceremony which gives the child the right to read the Vedas.

◄ Festivals are celebrated in India with great pomp and ceremony. Here, an elaborately decorated temple car is being drawn through the streets of Madurai. Statues of gods and goddesses can be seen inside the temple car.

▼ A Hindu wedding ceremony lasts several hours. The priest, bride and bridegroom sit around the sacred fire. The priest chants verses from the Vedas and keeps the fire alive by throwing clarified butter into it. At one stage, he ties the end of the bride's sari to the bridegroom's clothes. The marriage is finally solemnized when the bride and groom take seven steps around the sacred fire. Brides usually wear red saris and lots of jewellery.

A woman in a *burqah*. The *burqah* is worn ' Muslim women in purdah when they go t of the house. Purdah is the Muslim istom of making women live in a special ea of the house apart from men. The only en they are allowed to see are their isbands or close male relations. This istom used to be very widespread, even nong Hindus, but it is fortunately dying out.

A dead man lying on a stretcher ready to be rried to the cremation grounds. Hindus not use coffins. The funeral procession, d by the eldest son or nearest relative, is companied by loud wailing and beating breasts. The widow never takes part in e funeral ceremonies. At the cremation ounds the priest chants verses from the das and the chief mourner sets fire to the neral pyre. Hindus believe that fire nsports the dead person's soul to the iritual world. Three days after the emation, the ashes are collected. Within year they must be thrown into a river such the Ganges.

Education and language

▼ This little girl is learning to spin and will soon be helping to support her family. She is unlikely to receive an education. Though primary schooling is free and compulsory in most states, India does not force parents to send their children to school. It tempts them with free books, uniforms and midday meals.

A problem of communication

In a country as large as India, with 15 languages and over 1,000 dialects, communication can be difficult. Hindi, the most widely spoken language, is not even understood in the South, where they speak Dravidian languages and English.

After Independence, Hindi was made the official language. People who did not speak it were furious and riots and demonstrations broke out. As a compromise all children now learn Hindi, English and their mother tongue.

Before the British introduced English into India, Muslims studied Persian, Arabic and Urdu, while the Hindus were taught their local language and Sanskrit. Hindus soon started learning English to enter the Indian Civil Service. Muslims looked down on European culture and had to be persuaded to learn it.

India now has over 100 universities and many technical colleges. Indian institutes of technology enjoy a good reputation, and students from all over the world come to study.

In spite of their sheltered upbringing, Indian women train as engineers, architects, lawyers and scientists, and are not afraid to get their hands dirty.

Some years ago skilled engineers fou that there were not enough jobs for them India. Many left to work abroad. This k of situation worries the Indian governm as India cannot afford to pay very h salaries. Many doctors and scientists a leave to work abroad.

Schools for all

Nearly 70 per cent of Indians can bar read or write. Their "signature" on bottom of an official form is a thumb pri Noisy schools in the daytime give way studious adult classes in the evenings, as farmers laboriously print the letters of alphabet.

Television and radio should make task of educating the farmers easier. Th are programmes on health and farmi techniques, as well as entertainment. U fortunately the level of Hindi used in broadcasts is often too difficult for listeners to understand.

Radio and television Hindi is based new dictionaries written by Hindi a Sanskrit scholars. Instead of using an E lish word the scholars invent one using Sanskrit root. This often causes confusion

▼ It's an open air life in a village primary school! Two or three classes are held beside each other and children from the next class can be heard reciting their multiplication tables. The syllabus covers the three "Rs", hygiene and public health, Indian history, geography and physical training. Many children leave school at an early age and do not continue their education.

▲ Secondary schools prepare children for the school leaving examination at 17. Standards are high and children receive a lot of homework. Sometimes they learn the notes by heart. This method ot schooling la too much stress on passing examinations and does not always provide a good all-round education.

The increase in education

Indian children spend eight years in primary education. Secondary education lasts three years. They can then attend university or technical college. Since Independence there has been a dramatic rise in the numbers attending all educational levels.

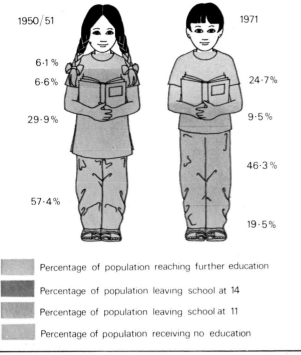

1950/51

6·1 %
6·6 %

29·9 %

57·4 %

1971

24·7 %

9·5 %

46·3 %

19·5 %

Percentage of population reaching further education

Percentage of population leaving school at 14

Percentage of population leaving school at 11

Percentage of population receiving no education

► The symbols of some of India's political parties. India is the largest democracy in the world but the majority of its people cannot read or write. They identify each party by its symbol on posters and on the ballot paper.

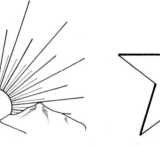

A university student asking a librarian help. Text books are in short supply and many students rely on library books. Indians want their children to go to university in te of overcrowding and poor facilities. degrees, even B.A. (failed) have a tain status.

► Most North Indian languages, like Hindi and Bengali are derived from Sanskrit, the mother of many Indo-European languages. Urdu, is the language of the Indian Muslims and has Persian, Arabic and Hindi words. It is written like Arabic. Tamil is a Dravidian language spoken in South India.

Some Indian scripts

HINDI

बच्चों का जन्म दिन

URDU

جھیل کے اس پار

BENGALI

ভারতের গৌরব

TAMIL

உள்ளம்கவர்கள்வன்

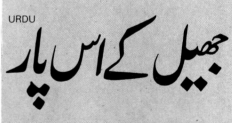

Preserving the jungle

Sunset, the screech of parakeets and roar of tigers. Deer and goats hurry f[e]fully from the watering holes, avoid snakes, panthers and leopards. This is popular image of the Indian jungle.

Unfortunately this picture is far fr true. Today, wild animals are under si from man. The Indian cheetah is exti[n]there are only about 200 Indian lions l and the famous Royal Bengal tiger is un sentence. The wildlife population of In is now only one-tenth of what it was years ago.

Hunting was one of the favourite sp[e]of the Maharajahs and the British offic Yet it is thanks to them that there are so wild animals left in India. To protect t[he]sport they introduced wildlife reserves a would only allow shooting during fi seasons. The main scourge of animal were poachers who hunted animals their skins and horns.

The government has established a W life Board to protect wild animals.

▲ A brooding lioness of the Gir forest. Thanks to the Maharajahs of Junagadh, this species is still alive. They were considered royal game in this state and so escaped indiscriminate hunting. To protect this severely depleted species, the Indian government has to compensate the villagers whose cattle the lions sometimes prey on.

▼ Aloof, the one-horned rhinoceros turns its back on the world. Over half the Indian rhinos live in the Kaziranga reserve. They are no longer used as front line "tanks" in warfare as they once were in ancient India. The Indian rhino never uses its horn when attacking. Instead it bites with the large incisors in its upper and lower jaws.

▲ In India the chital or spotted deer are mainly seen in the central and southern parts. They need to be very fast to avoid all their natural predators and packs of wild dogs which roam the forests. Chital are known for not sticking to seasons for mating or shedding antlers.

The peacock is India's national bird. Emperor Shah Jehan had a throne modelled on its glorious plumage. Peacocks shed their feathers once a year. These are much in demand for making fans and ornaments.

An elephant family on the move. Elephants are still used in India to shift logs or take visitors around the zoos and sanctuaries. When shifting logs, some elephants prefer to use one forefoot rather than the other, just like humans.

▶ The Royal Bengal tiger, once the king of the Indian jungle, is nearly extinct. Many hunters have written books about their experiences with man-eating tigers, yet tigers normally treat humans as unworthy, tasteless prey. They only become man-eaters if they are old, sick or injured. Tigers are nocturnal. To see them in their natural habitat, bait is laid in a clearing. The observers sit in platforms built in nearby trees. Sometimes days elapse before a tiger is seen.

Medicine and science

▲ This street pedlar is a combination of herbalist, quack doctor and conjurer. Many have faith in his potions and ointments. In the Fifties, a pharmaceutical company analysed one of these medicines sold as *pagal ki dawah* (medicine for madness). From it they isolated reserpine which was used to treat schizophrenia.

▼ A surgeon performing an operation in a Bombay hospital. Since Independence, India has built many new hospitals but most are still overcrowded and ill-equipped.

Medicine—old and new

Modern and traditional medicine survive side by side in India. When a person falls ill he has a wide choice of doctors. There are Western-style doctors trained in modern medicine, *vaids* trained in Ayurvedic medicine, *hakims* trained in Greek and Arab medicine, and homeopaths.

The *vaids* base their remedies on the herbs and potions described in the Vedas and in ancient medical texts such as the *Charaka Samhita*. The *hakims* use herbs or pastes made from pearls, precious stones and minerals. Both these forms of medicine are based on the balance of the humours: wind, blood, bile and phlegm.

Homeopaths try to make the body heal itself. They use tiny amounts of drugs which co-operate with the body's normal resistance to cure the disease.

Since 1947, India has given modern medicine top priority. Unfortunately, most doctors prefer to work in the cities where they earn better salaries. As a result village hospitals are understaffed. The government has plans to train people, including *vaids* and *hakims*, in basic medical techniques to deal with common ailments. This will leave village doctors free to treat the more serious cases.

India has made great progress in the control of epidemics. Cholera, typhoid and smallpox are almost under control, and vaccination against tuberculosis is widespread. Life expectancy at birth has risen from 32 to 50 years. Since more children now survive birth and live longer, people are being encouraged to use family planning, though they still have traditional prejudices against it.

Scientific developments

Ancient India's contributions to scie[nce] include the zero, the value of π, and algeb[ra]. From very early times Indians were usi[ng] the decimal system and algebra in th[eir] astronomical calculations. Today Ind[ian] scientists like the late C. V. Raman, w[ho] won the Nobel prize for his work on spect[ra] and the astrophysicist J. V. Narlikar, a[re] world famous.

As India is so dependent on the mo[n]soon, meteorological research is very [im]portant. Weather satellites have been s[et] up from the Thumba rocket station whi[ch] send back data on changes in the atm[os]phere. India has now made a satellite [at] Bangalore for further scientific research a[nd] is carrying out tests on the peaceful u[se] of nuclear power.

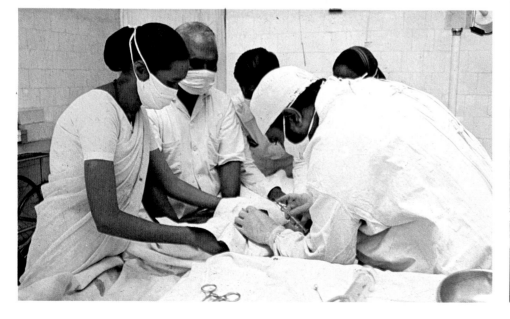

Yoga and meditation

◀ Yoga and meditation are popular in the West to relieve the strains of modern life. The girl sitting in the lotus pose of Hatha Yoga is starting the long process which teaches control over the body and mind. The final aim is to free the mind from distractions so that it can experience God.

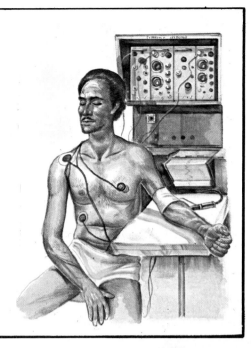

▶ Scientists have found that during meditation people's brain rhythms are altered. The traces are similar to those in a relaxed person just before sleep. Yogis can reduce their heart and pulse rates and can breathe very shallowly. As an experiment a few years ago, a yogi was buried several feet underground. He lived on the air in his coffin for many days.

◀ The strange geometrical shapes of the Jantar Mantar Observatory in Delhi. It was built in 1725 by the Rajput astronomer Maharajah Jai Singh. An Indian astronomer suggested in the fifth century A.D. that the earth moves around the sun. Astrology, considered a science in India, is based on the positions of the sun, the moon, the planets and stars. A person's destiny pivots on the time of his birth but he can overcome it by strength of will.

▶ This pillar near the Qutb Minar in Delhi demonstrates the ancient Indian skills in metal working. Modern science still cannot explain how the pillar, a single shaft of iron, has remained free from rust for over 1,500 years.

▼ The Bhabha Atomic Research Centre across the river at Trombay. The centre makes radioactive isotopes for the treatment of cancer and irradiates rice and groundnut seeds to produce better strains. In 1974 India exploded a nuclear device in the Rajasthan desert.

The plight of the farmer

▲ The bullock-drawn plough is used throughout India. Farms are often too small for tractors to be used. Many farms consist of small plots which are miles apart.
The government is trying to make the owners of such farms accept other land in exchange for their more distant plots.

The Green Revolution

Over 70 per cent of Indians depend on the land for a livelihood. Many of them eat only what the land produces and are ruled by the monsoon. If the monsoon is good, they have enough to eat; if it fails, they live on inadequate government aid.

Since 1947, India has built dams, canals and fertilizer factories and has started manufacturing its own agricultural equipment. Today, 50 per cent of the land is cultivated, but development is a slow process.

India hoped to be self sufficient in cereals by 1975. It imported a new kind of seed called Mexican dwarf which produced twice as much wheat as the older variety. Well-irrigated areas like the Punjab and Haryana doubled their crops and came to be known as the "granary of India". Similar rice seed, though less successful, was being tried in Tamil Nadu and Andhra Pradesh.

Unfortunately, the new seeds require large amounts of chemical fertilizers, good irrigation and modern methods of farming. Poorer farmers find it difficult to pay high world prices for seed and fertilizers.

A time for change

Under British rule, half the land w owned by *zamindars*, rich landowners w charged their tenant farmers high re Bad harvests meant borrowing to pay rent and tenants could seldom afford to their plots. The government abolished t system after Independence, placing a li on land ownership. Tenants are paid fi wages, and can rarely afford to buy th own land. Rich farmers get round th laws by bribery, and benefit most fr government aid.

India is still having to import gra seeds, fertilizers and machinery, and therefore having to modify its approach agriculture. Expensive dam-building c tinues, but is accompanied by the devel ment of local irrigation schemes. Th include sinking tube-wells and lining sn canals to prevent leakage. Animal man is widely used as fertilizer, and lo through pests and rats are being elimina Everything is being used as economically possible.

The Persian wheel is used to transfer water from a well to a canal. Two yoked bulls, moving in a tight circle, draw the water up from the well in pots. These rotate in the vertical wheel, depositing their contents into the canal. This primitive form of irrigation is used in many other parts of Asia.

▼ The Bhakra dam under construction. It symbolises India's agricultural achievements. Together with the nearby Nangal dam, it provides irrigation and hydro-electric power to the Punjab, Haryana and Rajasthan. India has built many dams since Independence, but lack of money is slowing down progress.

▲ Indian fishermen often use these huge "Chinese nets". They lay bait for the fish and draw up the nets when full. Modern techniques such as fish farming, developing better varieties of fish seed and sounding the ocean depths for fish have only just been introduced. India exports marine products all over the world.

Transplanting rice can be back-breaking work! The seeds are planted just before the monsoon. Once the shoots are 1-2 feet (30-61 cm) tall, they are transplanted to waterlogged fields. To keep the plots under water, they are surrounded by mud walls. The rice is harvested after six months.

This modern threshing machine saves valuable time. It is a far cry from the traditional method of making cattle trample over stalks to remove the grain. In India modern machinery is not used to save man-power, of which there is plenty, but to improve efficiency.

Myths, legends and heroes

► The god, Shiva, the Destroyer, doing the cosmic dance. This represents the natural rhythms of the Universe. His third eye shoots out deadly rays. Shiva is married to Parvati, who is often worshipped in the form of Kali. Their son, Ganesh, is the god of Prosperity. In a fit of rage, Shiva chopped off his son's head and the other gods replaced it with that of an elephant.

▼ The god Krishna playing the flute to a group of milkmaids. Each one thinks he is dancing with her alone. He is an incarnation of Vishnu and is one of the best loved Hindu gods. As a young man he was very mischievous. He teased the village girls and stole their clothes while they were swimming. His favourite was the beautiful Radha.

The Pandavas and the Kauravas

The epic poem *Mahabharata* is the story the five Pandava brothers who gamb away their kingdom to their cheati cousins, the Kauravas. One scene is a gr battle fought near Delhi.

Arjuna, the best warrior of the five, l heart at the thought of killing his cousi The god Krishna, who served as charioteer, lectured him on his duty as prince. Arjuna, refortified, helped to a nihilate the enemy. The epic poem *Bhaga Gita* consists of this lecture and summar some aspects of Hindu philosophy.

The Mountain Rat

The Moghul Emperor, Aurangzeb, call Shivaji the "Mountain Rat" because of wiliness. According to legend, Shivaji a his followers once surprised the enemy climbing a sheer rock face on the backs giant turtles. On another occasion, Shiv outwitted a Muslim general. They we supposed to meet for a peace treaty, u armed and with one attendant each. T general had a hidden dagger, but Shiv was gloved in steel tiger claws. As th embraced on meeting, Shivaji dise bowelled the general.

▲ Rama with his wife Sita, brother Lakshman, and Hanuman, the monkey god. Rama and Sita are the ideal Hindu couple. Rama's father was infatuated with his fourth wife. In a weak moment he promised to make her son king, and agreed to send his heir Rama to the forest for 14 years. Rama's adventures in the forest are described in the epic *Ramayana*.

Dressed in men's clothes and with her horse's reins clenched between her teeth, Lakshmibai, the Rani of Jhansi, leads her men into battle. This famous heroine of the Indian Mutiny is a symbol of the struggle for Indian Independence. When her husband died leaving her childless, the British claimed her kingdom for themselves. The Rani did not take this passively. She helped lead the Mutiny, determined to rid North India of the British presence. She fell in the thick of the fighting using her sword with both hands. The British did not realize they had shot her because of her male attire.

Yes, I sold my car. I find this cheaper.

◄ The bewildered taxi passenger in Laxman's cartoon represents the ordinary man in the street. Laxman's cartoons appear regularly in an Indian daily newspaper. These light-hearted pinpricks about Indian life are a source of embarrassment to the government. Laxman is regarded as the champion of the harassed and bemused Indian public.

▲ Vinobha Bhave is regarded as Mahatma Gandhi's spiritual heir. He believes in non-violence and peaceful revolution. In 1951 he began walking from village to village in India, asking landowners to give up some of their land to the poor. This Bhoodan movement, as it is called, had many followers but did not have very much success.

Curry and spice

Some like it hot

To be good a curry does not necessarily have to be hot. In fact too many chillies would ruin the subtle flavour of many Indian dishes. There is no one dish called curry, and the taste of Indian food varies by region and even by household.

Many South Indians are vegetarians and rice is their staple food. They breakfast on *idlis* (rice cakes) and *sambhar*, a dish made from lentils and vegetables. Their *dosas* are delicious rice-flour pancakes stuffed with spicy vegetables.

North Indian food shows a Muslim influence. People eat more meat, cook in *ghee* (clarified butter) and have *chapattis* instead of bread or rice. In their famous underground clay ovens, *tandoors*, meat is hung over the glowing coals on hooks.

People who live near the coast eat a lot of fish and seafood, and in Bombay you can eat the traditional Parsi dish *Patra ni Macchi*, fish wrapped in banana leaves.

Indian sweets are given as presents at all festivals. They are usually very sweet, sticky and highly flavoured.

Food customs

Food from another person's plate, or sips from his glass are *jhoota*, or impure. This caste taboo survives for hygienic reasons and helps prevent epidemics.

Hindus will not eat meat from the sacred cow and Muslims will not touch pork. In fact, all meat for Muslims must be slaughtered according to religious rules. During the month's fast of Ramadan, Muslims are forbidden to eat, drink water or smoke cigarettes before sundown. Indians eat with their right hand rather than using knives and forks. It is impolite to use the left hand.

Rich Indians still have retinues of servants to shop, cook, serve, and wash up. Traditional families insist on their being of the right caste.

The drinking of alcohol is not as widespread as in the West, although there are several strong local brews such as *feni* from Goa.

▲ A woman cooking the family's midday meal. She makes up the coal fire every morning and sometimes uses the bucket-shaped barbeque. The food is protected from flies and rodents in a cupboard with wire mesh sides. The cupboard legs stand in bowls of water to prevent insects from crawling in. Water, yoghurt and milk are kept cool in earthernware pots. City kitchens often have modern equipment.

Regional dishes

▲ The Gujarati housewife has a busy mealtime refilling the bowls on her guests' *thalis*. She can eat only after they have had their fill of the *dals* (lentils), vegetable curries, rice, *puris* and *pappadoms*.

▲ Spicy vegetarian dishes served on a disposable banana leaf. South Indian food is often thickened with grated coconut. It is usually very hot and eaten with rice and pickles.

▲ Barbecued tandoori chicken from North India. The distinctive colour and flavour come from the marinade of yoghurt, spices, and chillis. It is served with *nan* (bread) onion rings, lettuce and lemon wedges.

▲ *Maccher Jhol,* the famous fish dish of Bengal, has a subtle flavour of mustard oil. The rivers provide Bengalis with an abundance of fish. They believe this diet is good for the intellect.

A spice seller surrounded by heaps of red chilli powder, ground yellow turmeric and other spices. Indians use many spices in their cooking and make up a different spice for each dish. A good cook would never dream of using ready-mixed curry powder.

The pan wallah has many varieties of pan. Finely chopped betel nuts, lime paste, catechu and other spices are wrapped in the chosen pan leaf. Pan, which often has tobacco added to it, aids the digestion and stains the mouth red.

Cooking the Indian way

KORMA
680 g stewing meat, cut into cubes
225 g yoghurt
1 tablespoon cumin seeds, ground
1 teaspoon poppy seeds, ground
1 teaspoon red chilli powder
4-5 black pepper corns, ground
2-3 peeled cardamoms
3-4 cloves
3 cloves of garlic, crushed
1¼ cm square peeled ginger, crushed
450 g onions, cut into rings

Blend all ingredients together, except the meat and onions. Leave the meat to soak in this mixture for at least three hours. Fry the onions in oil until golden and add meat mixture. Add salt to taste. Cook for 1½ hours on medium heat. Garnish with coriander leaves.

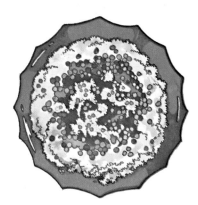

PEAS PILLAU
225 g Basmati or Patna rice
115 g frozen peas
2 cloves
2 peeled cardamoms
small piece of bayleaf
small piece of cinnamon
salt to taste

Wash the rice thoroughly until the water runs clear. Leave it to soak for 30 minutes. Drain, and cover the rice with 2½ times as much water. Add the spices and salt. Boil for 10-15 minutes until the rice is cooked. If it looks sticky, drain into a colander and steam it over boiling water. Fry the onions until crisp and toss the peas in the pan until they are warm. Add the cooked rice and stir everything together gently. Serve hot.

AUBERGINE BHARTA
900 g aubergines
450 g sliced onion rings
1 tablespoon powdered cumin seeds
3 tomatoes, finely chopped
225 g yoghurt
2-3 cloves of garlic, finely chopped
salt, pepper, green chillies to taste

Halve the aubergines lengthways, wrap in foil and bake in a medium oven for 45 minutes. When cool, peel and mash the flesh. Fry the onions until golden. Add the cumin and cook for two minutes. Add the aubergines and other ingredients. Serve hot.

COCONUT BARFI
1 litre milk
115 g desiccated or grated coconut
85 g sugar
2-3 peeled, crushed cardamom seeds
few drops of pink or green colouring

Bring the milk to the boil in a heavy saucepan and allow it to simmer until reduced to half. Stir constantly. Add the coconut, sugar and crushed cardamom seeds and continue stirring until very thick. Add the colouring to the mixture and pour it into a shallow greased dish. When it has set and cooled, cut into squares.

The market place

▲ One rupee, or 100 naya paisa, is worth about five British pence. Some rich Indians do not declare all their income. This hidden income, or "black money" is illegal and is usually spent on luxuries.

Shopping for the home

The Indian housewife can do most of daily shopping in the comfort of her o home. The butcher, fisherman and fr and vegetable sellers go from house house carrying their wares in baskets behi their bicycles. Each pedlar has a distinct call which can be heard several streets awa Sometimes they recite little verses advert ing their goods.

Once a week the housewife goes to market, where goods are generally cheap She haggles furiously with the stall own and usually manages to get her price. Ma housewives dislike going to the governm supermarkets where prices are fixed.

Conservationists

Presents and material for clothes are a bought at the market. The Indian tai will work in the house. Sometimes he w spend the whole day there doing fittin mending shirts, or remaking clothes.

Indians are natural conservationis Few goods are packaged and bottles returnable. Paper bags are made fr newspaper or old exercise books. Once month a rag-and-bone man comes round buy all the waste paper and empty bott Few people can afford to buy books keep. After they have read them they res them.

Foreign goods can only be brought i the country with a government imp licence. As a result there is a thriving bla market in foreign luxury goods such watches, radios and cassettes.

▲ Farmers haggling over the price of cattle at a market in Maharashtra. Cattle are highly prized because they are still used as beasts of burden. Indian cows, even though they are considered sacred, are very scrawny and produce little milk. New breeds are being imported to improve the stock.

▼ A crowded jewellers' alley in a typical bazaar. The hawker is carrying his wares in a basket on his head. Indian bazaars are divided into areas, with jewellers in one street, fruit sellers in another, clothes shops in a third and so on. Prices vary as the buyer is expected to bargain.

A hardware stall with pots and pans, buckets, stainless steel goods and plates. Indian utensils are built to last. Pedlars come round the houses to sharpen the kitchen knives. When pots and pans become discoloured they are treated with a special powder which leaves a shiny metallic film on the inside. This process is called *kalayi*.

▼ People with household ration books queueing outside government controlled shops. Wheat, rice and sugar are rationed. These shops also stock many other foods at fixed prices. Unfortunately food hoarders can create greater scarcities. Many of them stock up to sell later at a profit.

▲ A fruit seller with papayas, apples and pomegranates piled high around him. Sometimes the fruit is artificially coloured to make it look more appetising. The discerning housewife will refuse to buy any fruit without feeling it first and sniffing it to check its quality.

▼ Many Indians are vegetarian and are lucky to have such a wide choice of fruit and vegetables. Indian vegetables have a strong flavour because they are not treated with insecticide. Housewives will buy their food fresh and in season because most of them cannot afford refrigerators.

BOTTLE GOURD

SNAKE GOURD

JACKFRUIT

BANANAS

PAPAYA

LIMES

SWEET POTATO

AUBERGINES

OKRA

GREEN CHILLIES

Bombay, a bustling metropolis

The commercial capital of India

Ships and aircraft from all over the world offload passengers and commodities in Bombay, and depart laden with India's exports. Whirring textile mills produce bales of cotton, while business men negotiate last minute deals in their air-conditioned offices.

Bombay is the capital of Maharashtra, but its inhabitants, Gujaratis, Goans and foreign tourists have created a new culture which is typical only of Bombay.

The richer Indians live in the residential area of Malabar Hill. They are the fashion trend-setters for the rest of India. Their lives revolve around the clubs where they swim and play golf and bridge, and the race course where women in glorious saris place bets on the day's favourite. In the evenings they frequent the fashionable restaurants or visit the latest discotheque.

Bombay is also the home of the Parsees, Persian refugees who fled persecution in the seventh century A.D. They believe fire is a sacred manifestation of God and worship in "Fire Temples". When they die their bodies are placed in the Towers of Silence in Malabar Hill, where hordes of vultures pick the bones clean.

The other side

Bombay's colourful bazaars are always crowded. Jhaveri Bazaar has beautiful gold and silver jewellery and Kalbadevi sells the products of the nearby cotton mills. In Chor Bazaar (Thieves Market) one can buy back one's stolen property. Colaba, near the army cantonment, is a fashionable shopping area.

The city houses India's thriving Hindi film industry, and during film premieres crowds gather outside the cinemas to see their favourite film stars.

As with most cities there is another side to Bombay. Every day sees strikes and food, water and housing shortages. Many people, including some office workers, live and sleep on the pavements. Beggars abound. In spite of all this, no Bombayite would willingly live anywhere else.

▲ The gateway of India stands proudly overlooking one of the world's finest natural harbours. The Gateway was built as a triumphal arch for George V's visit to India in 1911.

◀ Dhobis washing Bombay's dirty linen at the *dhobi ghat*. The clothes are boiled, soaped and then beaten on rock slabs. After drying in the sun, they are pressed with huge metal irons.

▼ Marketing the catch at the Sassoon fish docks. Every day the fishing fleet of dhows and other small boats bring in enough fresh fish to feed Bombay's six million inhabitants

The sandy public beach at Chowpatty. Vendors of coconuts, icecream, bhelpuri and other spicy snacks do a roaring trade. Crowds gather here for rallies. During the festival of Ganesh Chaturthi, family processions carry garlanded images of the god, Ganesh, into the seas.

▼ Victorian gothic architecture, like that of the Municipal Corporation building and the Victoria Terminus railway station, can be seen in Bombay. These large, cool buildings are relics of the British raj. Unlike modern skyscrapers, these buildings do not require air-conditioning.

▲ Bombay's hot "meals on wheels" service at lunchtime. Office workers' wives prepare their lunch in the morning and put it into insulated containers called tiffin carriers. These are delivered, amazingly to the right office, on handcarts. They add further confusion to the congested traffic.

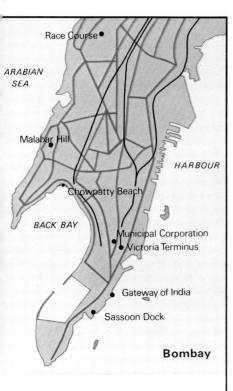

Seven tiny islets join together to form the island of Bombay. Bombay was once a tiny fishing village owned by the Portuguese. In 1661, it was given to Charles II of England. Today it has an international airport and is a major Asian seaport.

The Moghuls

▼ Throughout his life, Akbar's armies were at war in different parts of India. They were either in Rajasthan putting down the militant Rajputs, or in Bengal, Bihar and Orissa taking new territories. Akbar's attempts to penetrate the Deccan met with less success and he never ventured beyond the river Kistna.

Babur's destiny

Babur, a descendant of Genghis Khan and Timur the Lame, felt destined to conquer India. He invaded India from Kabul five times in seven years. Finally in 1526, at the Battle of Panipat, he became the first Moghul emperor. His reign in Agra was uneasy. The Rajput warrior kings, who banded together to expel him, attacked continuously.

Humayun, Babur's son, was too fond of pleasure to keep the empire for long. After ten years rule, he was defeated and only regained his kingdom a few months before his death.

Akbar the Great

Babur's grandson, Akbar the Great, was a wise and just ruler. He defeated the Rajp

Akbar's empire 1556-1605

Kabul
KASHMIR
Lahore
BALUCHISTAN
SIND
RAJPUTANA · Delhi
Umarkot
Chitor
BENGAL
Calcutta
GUJARAT
I N D I A
ORISSA

▲ Babur, the first Moghul, was a learned and just emperor. When his son, Humayun, fell ill he begged God to exchange his life for his son's. Humayun recovered and Babur died shortly afterwards.

▶ Akbar and his courtiers crossing a river on elephants. He was an adventurous youth and chafed under the supervision of his regent Bairam Khan. He dismissed his regent and became king two years later, at twenty.

nces and then won them over by giving
m high posts in his administration. His
ourite general was the Rajput, Raja Man
gh. Akbar also married a Rajput
ncess.

Akbar was a great warrior and only met
match in two adversaries, Maharana
tap of Mewar and Chand Bibi, the
ve Queen of Ahmednagar.

Akbar removed discrimination against
n-Muslims by abolishing *jizya*, a special
which all of them had to pay, and for-
de the enslaving of prisoners of war. With
help of Raja Todar Mull, a Rajput
nce, he developed a new tax system.

Akbar was fascinated by religion and
rted his own called the Din-il-illahi. It
s a mixture of Hinduism, Islam and
roastrianism.

Akbar's successors were less imposing.
hangir was a patron of the arts. He loved
wife, Nur Jehan, deeply and eventually
was in control of the empire. Shah
han is remembered for the Taj Mahal in
ra, and the Red Fort and Jumma Masjid
Delhi. Aurangzeb extended the empire
t he was disliked, particularly for re-
posing the *jizya*.

Akbar overjoyed at the birth of his heir
hangir. Jehangir led an unsuccessful
bellion against his father. He was kept
der house arrest until his pardon, a few
onths before Akbar's death.

▲ Servants carrying a dead lioness back
from the hunt. Akbar, like all the Moghuls,
loved hunting. Although he was almost
illiterate, he enjoyed the company of poets
and artists. The singer, Tansen, one of the
"nine gems" of his court sang so beautifully
that even animals were said to listen.

▼ The Taj Mahal is made of marble and
inlaid with semi-precious stones. It was
Shah Jehan's memorial to his wife
Mumtaz Mahal. The black tomb he planned
for himself was never built. He died
imprisoned by his son, gazing at the image
of the Taj Mahal in a small mirror in his prison.

The British raj

Company rule

In 1600, Queen Elizabeth I of England granted the East India Company a charter to trade with India. The Company soon became involved in Indian politics and developed control by playing off one petty Indian ruler against another. By the mid-nineteenth century there were effectively two Indias, British and Indian. The British maintained control over the Indian rulers through their Residents or political agents.

Discontent over British rule came to a head in 1857, during the Indian Mutiny. This savage conflict was sparked off by the sepoys (Indian soldiers in the army) on the introduction of the Enfield rifle. The cartridges had to be bitten off before firing, and the sepoys believed they were coated with the fat from pigs and cows. To touch them was against the religion of both Hindus and Muslims, and they mutinied. Terrible atrocities were committed by both sides. Although it did not bring an end to British rule, the Mutiny diminished the East India Company's power. A Viceroy was appointed by the British throne to rule India.

The jewel of the Empire

The British now felt greater responsibility towards India. With an efficient civil service they built roads, railways, harbours and a telegraph system.

Indians such as Raja Ram Mohan Roy were influenced by British thinkers. Roy's liberal views changed Hinduism. He helped to abolish *sati*, the Hindu custom of burning widows on their husband's funeral pyre.

By the turn of the century, pressure for Independence was growing. The Indian National Congress, founded as a political discussion group, led the struggle. The British gave some freedom but divided Indian voters by religion, arousing traditional suspicions between Hindus and Muslims. Tensions between these two communities came to a head at Independence, and two countries were created—India, and the Muslim state of Pakistan.

Vasco da Gama

In 1498, Vasco da Gama, a Portuguese explorer, sailed around Africa and opened the sea route to India. By 1700 all the major European powers were fighting for trading posts in India. The British East India Company was established in Bombay, Calcutta and Madras; the Portuguese in Goa; the French in Pondicherry and the Dutch in Negapatam.

The two main rivals were the French and the British. They extended their power by siding with Indian rulers in return for trade concessions. The siege of Arcot in 1754, put an end to French dominance.

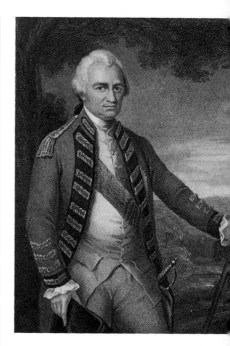

▲ Robert Clive, a clerk in the East India Company, rose to be Governor of Bengal. After defeating Siraj ud Daulah at Plassey, Bengal, in 1757 he made his general, Mir Jaffar, the Nawab. With Clive's help, the British gained control of Bengal, Bihar and Orissa.

▼ Sepoys moving into battle during the Indian Mutiny. This bloodthirsty conflict was caused by British disregard for Indian customs and needs. The Indian army turned against the British, massacring hundreds in Kanpur. The mutiny was finally broken at the Siege of Lucknow in 1858.

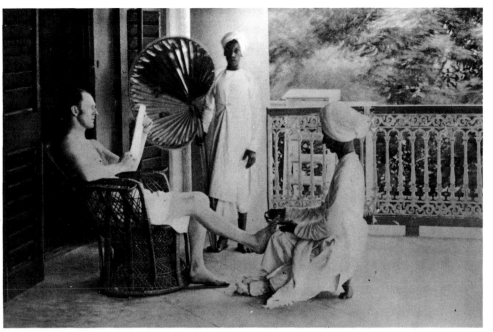

◄ The Victoria Memorial in Calcutta. Queen Victoria was crowned Empress of India in 1877, twenty years after the Indian Mutiny. Her son Edward VII came to India in 1876 to prepare the way for her coronation. He held court in Delhi and was lavishly entertained by the Maharajahs, all of whom swore loyalty to the British Crown.

▲ The British officer and his wife became very used to the luxury of Indian life. The *memsahib* was totally dependent on her servants and found it difficult to adjust to British life on their return. Many British stayed on in India after retirement. Some of them were interested in Hinduism and translated the religious texts into English.

▼ Polo was a favourite pastime for off-duty British officers. They learnt the game from the Maharajahs, and taught them to play cricket. They spent many afternoons with their families at the "Club", drinking, swimming and playing sports.

▲ During British rule, Indian Nawabs and Maharajahs commanded absolute loyalty from their followers. Although heavily taxed by the British, their riches, accumulated over centuries, were well safe-guarded. At the turn of the century, many sent their children to be educated at British public schools.

The struggle for freedom

A new vision

The Mahatma (Great Soul) gave a new meaning to non-violence. He said that anything gained through violence was not worth having.

Born Mohandas Karamchand Gandhi in Gujarat in 1869, he qualified as a lawyer in England before practising in South Africa. During his life he often went to jail, cheerfully, for disobeying unfair laws. He called this disobedience *Satyagraha*—the force of truth.

Gandhi returned to India in 1914 and joined Congress leaders in the struggle for Independence after the Jallianwalla bagh massacre. General Dyer had opened fire on a trapped, unarmed crowd. Hundreds of Indians were killed.

Following Gandhi's lead, the Indian National Congress organized a peaceful boycott of the British. All over the country, people burnt their British goods, especially cloth. They wore clothes made from *khadi*, handmade Indian cotton. In protest against the salt tax they collected their own salt from the sea. Nearly 30,000 Indians were proud to go to jail in the name of Independence.

Freedom, partition and assassination

The end of the Second World War brought a Labour government to Britain, sympathetic to the Indian cause. By now the nationalist movement had split. Jinnah, the leader of the Muslim league, asked for Pakistan as a separate country for the Muslims.

In 1946, fierce rioting broke out between Hindus and Muslims in North India. Lord Mountbatten, the last Viceroy, sent to dismantle British power, was forced to agree to Partition. India and Pakistan gained Independence on August 15th, 1947.

Partition bought in its wake the largest massacres known outside war. Thousands of Hindus and Muslims were killed. Gandhi succeeded in quelling the rioting, but was assassinated weeks later by a Hindu bigot, for his defence of the Muslims. At his funeral, Jawaharlal Nehru, the Indian Prime Minister, said "The light has gone out of our lives, and there is darkness everywhere".

▼ As a young man Gandhi wore Western clothes. Later he began to wear the *dhoti* because it was all the average Indian could afford. Though a deeply religious man, he had no time for caste or ritual. He championed the cause of the untouchables and brought women into politics.

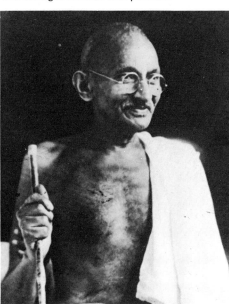

▲ In 1927 the Simon Commission came to India to study the changed political situation. Since there was not a single Indian in the group, it was boycotted by the Indian National Congress.

▼ Gandhi and Sarojini Naidu, the Bengali Congress leader, on their way to a Round Table conference. These unsuccessful discussions were held in London.

▼ Indira Gandhi, the daughter of Nehru and India's first woman Prime Minister, with Abdul Ghaffar Khan. He was known as the "frontier Gandhi" for his non-violent struggle against the British on the North-West frontier. After Partition, he wanted a separate state for the Pathans, and was jailed by the Pakistan government. He was given an enthusiastic welcome in India when he was released from prison in 1969.

▲ Jawaharlal Nehru, India's first Prime Minister, addressing the nation on the eve of Independence. He said "We made a tryst with Destiny . . . At the stroke of the midnight hour, when the World sleeps, India will awake to life and freedom".

▼ Gandhi's memorial in Delhi reflects the simplicity of his life. His last words as he lay dying from an assassin's bullet were "Hai Ram" (Dear God). They are sculpted in Hindi and are the only decoration on his humble monument.

Art, a gift of the gods

A shared experience

The god Shiva, as he danced to the rhythm of the Universe, is said to have given the world the seven notes of the musical scale. Since then arts have been considered "the language of the Gods". The artist combines sound, colour, rhythm, or gesture to arouse strong feelings in the audience. These feelings include Love, Terror, Anger and Humour, and are called *rasas*. There are nine basic *rasas* which, like the colours of the rainbow, can be combined by an artist to draw an image in the mind. Indian music and dance are the purest example of this technique.

All the classical forms of Indian dance follow these traditions. Every gesture has a meaning, but a great dancer can project a meaning and become the gesture. In addition to the ritual poses, the dancer must express the pure joy of movement and rhythm. Indian folk dancing is much simpler. The main elements of its beauty are this joy and rhythm, combined with the glorious local costumes.

In Indian music the mood is set by the *raga* or melody, and the *tala* or rhythm. Indian music is perhaps closest, in Western terms, to an imaginative solo where constantly changing rhythms are applied to a single phrase of music.

Living stone

From the bronze figurines of Mohenjo-Daro to the graceful natural carvings adorning the pillars in Indian caves and temples, Hindu sculpture has been able to generate a sense of movement.

Bronze representations of Shiva's cosmic dance were made, during the reign of the Cholas in South India, using the lost wax process. The image was first modelled in wax, then covered with clay. After the clay had hardened, the wax was melted out and molten metal poured in. When the metal had set, the mould was broken and the image polished and burnished.

Murals, miniatures and literature

In the prehistoric caves at Mirzapur, there are exciting paintings of the hunt, with wounded animals goring their pursuers. However the main stimulus to Indian art has been religion. The gigantic murals of the Ajanta caves show scenes of Buddhist life at the time.

By the fifteenth century A.D., artists were using paper and were able to make m[ore] elaborate illustrations. The miniatures [of] the Moghul and Rajasthani schools [are] world famous.

Hindu literature consists largely of po[etry] from the epics, and other religious te[xts.] Indian literature flowered during the l[ate] Moghul period, when Urdu, a sophistica[ted] language combining Persian, Arabic a[nd] Hindi, was widely spoken. Ghalib, who [was] a brilliant irreverent poet, wrote ve[rses] about the joys of wine and love. Just bef[ore] Independence Indian writers were fi[lled] with fervour. The Bengali, Rabindra[nath] Tagore won the Nobel prize for his w[ork] *Gitanjali*. He also wrote the Indian Natio[nal] Anthem.

▲ The love story of Krishna and Radha wa[s] a favourite theme for the miniature painters of the Rajasthani School. The figures are a[ll] two-dimensional and the most important person is the largest. Three artists often worked together on the same painting. One artist sketched the outline on primed paper, another coloured in the broad detail, while the master added the eyes and the expressions.

◄ Elaborately costumed Kathakali dancers act out episodes from the legends of the epic poems. The green-faced men are the heroes. The ones with a red knife-shaped scar on their faces are the villains. There is n[o] need for words. Their flashing eyes and ha[nd] gestures conjure up any image — from towering rage to flowers dancing in the breeze, or a startled deer in the forest.

This woman has painted a picture of [K]ali on the wall of her house. She hopes [it] will keep away evil spirits. This form of [fo]lk art has influenced many modern painters, [w]ho admire its simplicity.

▲ Playing the seven-stringed veena, an instrument which can be made to sound like the human voice. Indian music is often strange to Western ears because it concentrates on melody.

▲ The soaring gateways of the Meenakshi temple at Madurai were added after the simple temple had been built. South Indian architecture differs from the Moghul beauty of the Taj Mahal, with its onion-shaped domes. It can be recognised by the series of sawn-off pyramids built one on top of the other.

◄ Hindu temples such as those at Khajuraho, Konarak and Mahabalipuram are full of sculpture. Pillars and walls are covered with statues of gods, people and animals. The Muslim religion forbids sculpture in mosques. They are decorated with verses from the Koran, geometric patterns or flowers, all inlaid into the stone.

Time for leisure

Festivals

There are over a dozen public holidays in the Indian calendar. People of all religions join together to celebrate each other's festivals.

Two of the most popular festivals are Holi and Diwali. Holi is a fertility festival and celebrates the frolics of the mischievous god Krishna. Children fill bicycle pumps with coloured water and spray it at anyone within range. People are not allowed to object so they wear old clothes.

Diwali, the festival of lights, is celebrated in October. Tiny earthenware pots are filled with oil, and a wick made of cotton wool is set alight. These are used to decorate the houses and the night is filled with loud bangs and fireworks.

The main Muslim festival is Id-ul-Fitr which comes at the end of the month's fast of Ramadan. Everyone wears new clothes and, as is the custom with most festivals, the older generation give the children money. There are always sweets and spicy food to help along the festivities.

Indian sports

Like people all over the world, Indians lov[e] sport. The favourite sports are cricke[t] hockey and football. In the afternoons [in] the cities, hundreds of people swarm all ov[er] the *maidans*, or public playing fields.

Indians have been world champions [at] hockey, have won the tennis Davis Cu[p] and are good at cricket and football. The[re] are few professional sportsmen and th[e] government is far behind most countries i[n] its support of sport.

There are many Indian sports which a[re] not well-known. Kabbaddi is a sport simila[r] to team wrestling. One player runs into h[is] opponents' territory holding his breath. H[e] has to touch as many of the other side [as] possible, before taking another breath. The[y] try to hold him and if he can return to h[is] side, all those he has touched are out.

The kite-flying season occurs just befo[re] the monsoon. Kite fights can becom[e] vicious. Children often try to cut down the[ir] rivals' kites by covering their kite strin[g] with powdered glass.

▲ A deadly cobra sways out of its basket, intrigued by the snake charmer's *bin*. Contrary to popular belief, there are only four poisonous types of snake in India. If a house becomes infested with snakes, the snake charmer brings his mongoose round which attacks and kills the snakes.

▶ Eye-catching posters advertise the latest films. The growing Indian film industry is already larger than Hollywood. Most films are simple love stories and have song and dance sequences. Kissing on the screen is permitted. Indians are keen film-goers. They follow the exploits of their favourite film stars with interest in the film magazines.

▼ Giant effigies of Ravana and his brothers are burnt every year at Dussehra. On this day, Rama, king of Ayodhya, defeated Ravana, the wicked king of Sri Lanka who had stolen his wife. The monkey god, Hanuman, helped by setting fire to Sri Lanka with his tail.

Wrestling is popular all over India. Every age or town takes pride in its local restler. Competitions are held to see which e is the greatest. Dara Singh who oresented the Punjab is now an almost jendary figure. In the Olympic Games dian wrestlers have won gold medals.

▲ The Indian cricket team playing in a Test Match in London. Indian cricketers have played successfully all over the world. Ranjitsinhji was a prolific batsman during the time of W. G. Grace. In the old days the national team was often made up of princes who had been educated in England.

▲ The story teller is revered by Indian villagers. He entertains them with tales from epics and historical romances. A story teller once taught a king's son the art of government by using the *Jatakas,* ancient Buddhist stories. Aesop's fables are based on these stories.

45

Industry and crafts

▶ An engineer repairing a fault in a petro-chemical plant. India's petrochemical industries produce synthetic fibres, plastics, and other products. Since 1976 the rich offshore Bombay oilfield has been in commercial production. India hopes to be self-sufficient by 1990.

▼ Iron ore is mined in central and eastern India where whole towns have built up around the industry. New factories produce heavy machinery, railway wagons, and agricultural equipment.

The vital need for industry

Under British rule, India was exploited colony. Ships were used to exchange Ind raw materials for expensive manufactu British goods. In India local crafts langu ed and few factories were built. Howe some Indians like Jamshedji Tata real the need for industry. He set up the to ship of Jamshedpur in 1911 to house Ind main iron and steel mills with all its work

Post-Independence India needed to b up industry in record time. A program of five year plans was set up to deve natural resources. Top priority was provide the energy to run India's indust and huge dams were built to gene hydro-electric power. In the second year plan, large iron and steel works w built and the vast mineral resource Bihar were mined for iron ore, coal, cop and manganese.

Much of India's heavy industry is s owned. The private sector consists of a large organizations like Tatas, whose ind trial empire ranges from soap-making locomotive building, together with m medium and small scale industries. Fore businesses can only be set up if spe knowledge is needed, and there must b discrimination against Indians being ployed in the higher positions.

India is trying to become self-suffici It manufactures its own ships, diesel gines, machine tools, cars, pharmaceuti and films. Thousands of bicycles are sembled by individuals in tiny workshop Ludhiana.

Reviving village crafts

Many villagers earn extra money throu local crafts. In the old days they were ru lessly exploited by unscrupulous busin men. Today the government buys th products at fixed prices and sells them special emporiums in the major towns a cities. They also export them to earn In valuable foreign exchange.

Indian craftsmen make gold and sil jewellery and finely worked metal tra bowls and cups. Small marble boxes inl with stones are very popular and the ha made leather sandals are comfortable a hardwearing.

Indian textiles such as cashmere, mus silk and cotton are world famous. Bana silk is so delicate it is almost transpare The tie-and-dye work of Rajasthan justly famous for its richly-colou patterns.

▼ A man inlaying bits of bone and ivory into a carved wooden tray. Inlay work in wood, ebony and marble is popular in India for picture frames, cigarette cases and other household articles. Many of these products are exported to Indian shops abroad.

A Rajasthani woman embroidering pieces of mirror into brightly coloured materials. Each part of India is famous for a different style of embroidery. Kashmiri shawls are noted for their delicate patterns of clusters of flowers and birds with many-coloured plumage.

▲ This relatively modern textile dyeing factory uses synthetic dyes. In the old days Indians used vegetable and stone dyes and indigo which they exported all over the world. Each colour was significant. Green stood for youth and life, red for joy and happiness, and blue for peace.

▼ Spinning coir fibres from the hairs of the dried husk of the coconut. The yarn is used to make floor matting and string. In Kerala, which produces 90 per cent of India's coir, this kind of work is done by women in their own homes. They then sell it to the government at fixed prices.

Bullock carts, bicycles and Boeings

Cheap travel

In an Indian traffic jam at a level crossing one may see 5,000 years of transport history. Bullock carts and taxis jostle bicycles and scooters. Horse-drawn carriages, cars, lorries and buses clamour for the gates to be lifted. The jumbo jet flying overhead can barely be heard.

India's rail network, the world's fourth largest, carries coal, iron ore, steel, cement, food grains and fertilizers. The number of passengers carried daily amounts to more than the population of Switzerland. Third class travel is cheaper than anywhere else in Asia. For five British pence one can travel about 50 kilometres (31 miles). Most locomotives are still steam driven, but electrification and diesel engines are being introduced.

India has Asia's second largest merchant navy and 200 of its fleet of 260 ships are engaged in overseas trade. A special shipping line, called the Mogul line, ferries thousands of Muslims to Saudi Arabia on their way to Mecca.

Few people outside the cities can afford to run private cars. They rely on bicycles, bullock carts or State transport to get them around. The state buses link towns and villages, leaving a trail of dust and fumes on the slower traffic.

Bicycle jams

In Delhi, families can be seen riding around on bicycles. One child sits on the handlebars, the wife rides pillion with the baby, while the husband pedals furiously. The early morning bicycle jams, as clerks advance on the government buildings, are a sight to be seen.

India's roads are nationalized. The government builds rubble or *kaccha* roads to connect distant villages, rather than showpiece motorways.

Pedestrians, even in the cities, act as if they own the road. They will only be nudged out of the way by an overtaking horse or bullock.

▲ Horse-drawn carts are used to carry goods and people. Tongas (horse-drawn carriages) are still used in some of the bazaars but are being replaced by the faster scooter taxi, a two-seater carriage drawn by an ordinary scooter.

◀ Bombay's double decker buses are an efficient exception in the road transport system. They are a far cry from the dusty state transport buses.

▼ Rush hour commuters need to be agile get to work! The cool breeze, once the tra gets under way, can be quite a relief. As cities grow larger, cheap accommodation can only be found on the outskirts and passengers have to commute longer distances.

Air India

Air India, India's national airline, could be said to have pioneered the concept of luxury flights. Exceptional service and the palatial Indian decor of the Jumbo jets have won it many prizes. The smiling Maharajah symbol is now known in the 27 countries which are served by Air India's fleet of Boeing 747s and 707s.

Indian Airlines, the domestic service, provides links between the major cities and some neighbouring countries such as Bangladesh, Sri Lanka and Nepal. It operates 76 flights daily, carrying both passengers and freight.

◄ Barges provide a peaceful way of travelling from village to village. They carry goats, chickens, fish and village produce as well as passengers.

▼ Rajasthani village women are trained from childhood to carry heavy articles on their heads. This may be one of the reasons why they walk so gracefully.

◄ Bullock carts are the most common form of transport in India. Some carts are now fitted with rubber tyres to help them ride more easily. Cars and lorries may be kept to walking pace behind a bullock cart taking a family to market. The bullocks wear bells to warn off pedestrians.

India's impact on the world

◄ Ravi Shankar on sitar with Alla Rakha on tabla (drum) and an artiste on tampura. The seven basic notes of the Indian scale can be traced back to 1200 B.C. in the singing of the Vedas, and they were said to have been given by the god Shiva himself. Ravi Shankar is one of the few Indian musicians willing to experiment by including some features of Western music. He has played with Yehudi Menuhin, the famous violinist, as well as jazz and pop groups.

▶ Indian gypsies travelling to a fair. Gypsies are believed to have originated in India, and their culture throughout the world has roots in Hinduism. Sara, the Black Virgin they revere, is probably another manifestation of Kali, the black goddess of Destruction. Gypsies have a strict caste system with each family following the same jobs, and there are many Indian words in their Romany language.

▼ Satyajit Ray was the first of the new wave of Indian film directors who broke away from the box-office formula Indian films. Starting with *Pather Panchali* (Ballad of the Road), his quiet lyrical films show the problems of poverty, unemployment and social change in India. He does not give easy answers, only love and hope.

A philosophy of peace

India's culture has spread to all corners of the globe. It has influenced people's minds, bodies and souls. Imagine mathematics without the zero, or eating food without pepper. Nowadays more and more people are turning towards Indian religions and philosophy to find a deeper meaning to their lives.

Naturally, the country most influenced is Britain, which has had close contact with India over three centuries. Many words such as *jungle* and *bungalow* have become part of the English vocabulary. The word *jodhpurs* comes from the dress which the Maharajah of Jodhpur wore while riding.

A survey conducted in Britain in the Sixties showed that curry was the most popular meal when eating out. Indian restaurants can be found in almost any town in England and many shopkeepers now stock Indian chillies and spices.

Gandhi's example of non-violence and peaceful demonstration has influenced Civil Rights movements throughout the world. Martin Luther King in America and Albert Luthuli in South Africa both used his techniques in fighting for their people. In Britain thousands of people marched peacefully under the banner of the Campaign for Nuclear Disarmament to protest against the bomb.

The swinging Indian Sixties

During the Sixties "pop" culture took on an Indian flavour. Groups such as the Beatles became interested in Indian religions and music. They adopted an Indian Guru, and their fans took to meditation. Clothes were made from Indian materials and Indian fashions became popular.

Many people started communes based on Indian *ashrams*, where people with similar beliefs live together. As in India they practise meditation, grow their own food and live off simple village crafts. Nowadays a growing interest in the world's food problems and worries about being overweight have made Yoga and vegetarianism more fashionable.

In the Sixties, India struck a blow for women's rights when Indira Gandhi was elected its first woman Prime Minister.

The non-aligned bloc

Since Independence, India has shown other countries that it is not necessary to side with either the Soviet or the Western power blocs. This group of countries are said to be non-aligned, and act as a moderating influence in international politics. Indian army units have been sent by the United Nations for peace-keeping operations in the Congo and the disputed Arab-Israeli territory.

▼ Indians cheering their cricket team's victory in a Test series in London. Since the Second World War, many have come to work in Britain and become British citizens. It is said that without Indian doctors the British health service would break down.

▲ Queuing outside an Indian rice shop in Dar es Salaam in Tanzania. Indian traders have travelled all over the world, from Africa to the West Indies and Malaysia. Recently Uganda expelled many Indians. They were unpopular because they monopolized trade.

▲ Buddhism has the largest following of any religion on Earth. From 261 B.C. Ashoka sent missionaries to Egypt, Macedonia and the Near East. The Chinese traveller, Fa Hsien, visiting India in the fifth century A.D., returned to China with the sacred texts. From China, Buddhism spread throughout Eastern Asia. Although modified, the Eight-fold Path to Righteousness was followed universally.

Modern India

A new era

After Independence, India was faced with the immense problems of famine, poverty, epidemics, lack of industry and poor education. In Jawaharlal Nehru, India had a leader of vision to steer it along its difficult course.

Today, the Indian constitution protects the rights of all citizens. New reforms give women more rights in marriage, divorce and inheritance. The caste system is breaking down and fewer marriages are arranged. More people now marry for love. Indian people are still very poor by Western standards and can afford few luxuries.

A programme of five year plans has been developed to exploit India's natural resources and as industry progresses, people have a wider choice of jobs. Education and medicine have reached remote corners of the country.

Indian politics

In 1947, two-fifths of India was ruled by maharajahs who had to be persuaded to join the federation. All of them did, though Kashmir, with a large Muslim population, remains a cause of disputes between India and Pakistan.

Jawaharlal Nehru directed India's foreign policy towards peace and non-alignment, but today people question India's role as a peaceful nation. Recently it has taken Goa from the Portuguese, been involved in border conflicts with China and Pakistan and helped Bangladesh to gain its independence. It now has the potential to make nuclear weapons. India's attitude towards criticism of these activities might be summed up as "Peace yes, but not passivity".

In 1975 the government declared a state of emergency, saying that strong measures were needed to impose law and order and to strengthen the economy. The emergency was so unpopular that at the next elections, in 1976, for the first time, the Congress party was replaced in power by the Janata party.

By 1980 the Indian people were dissatisfied by their performance and voted Indira Ghandi and her "Indira Congress" party back into power.

▲ This woman roadside worker is scarcely striking a blow for women's liberation. Village women have always done hard manual labour in India. Since education became widespread, however, they have reached high positions in politics and government.

▶ Clocking in at a textile mill. Many Indian workers belong to trade unions. The unions resist automation if it displaces workers from their jobs. India's large work force and the adaptation of modern techniques give strength to its industry.

▼ India's pride as a nation can be seen during the vast Republic Day parades. Schoolgirls and soldiers, tanks and aeroplanes, file past the crowds. India became a Republic on January 26th 1950 but chose to remain within the Commonwealth.

◀ Contrasts such as this are inevitable in a developing country. Bombay has expanded so fast in recent years that there is an acute housing shortage. Attempts are being made to rehouse the shanty dwellers.

▼ Part of the world's largest democracy exercising its right of protest. Recently there have been many demonstrations in India against rising prices, food shortages and government corruption and bureaucracy.

▼ Thanks to the Green Revolution standards of living have risen sharply in areas like the Punjab. Peasants own tractors, have cars in their courtyards and there are petrol pumps at either end of the village. People eat better and live better. Other parts of India are making more gradual progress.

Reference
Human and physical geography

FACTS AND FIGURES

Full title: Bharat Ganrajya (Republic of India).
Capital: Delhi (4,065,698).
Position: Southern Asia between 8 04′ and 37 06′N and 68 07′ and 97 25′E. India has borders with Afghanistan, Pakistan, China, Nepal, Bangladesh and Burma.
Constituent parts: 22 States and 9 Union territories including the Andaman and Nicobar Islands and Lakshadweep.
Area: 3,287,782 sq. km.
Population: Estimated 683 million (1981). About 638 million in 1979.
Religion: Hindus (83 per cent); Muslims (11 per cent); Sikhs (2 per cent); Christians (2 per cent); Buddhists, Jains, Zoroastrians and other religions (2 per cent).
Political system: Parliamentary democracy based on national elections.
International organisations: India is a non-aligned country. It has special treaties of friendship, peace and co-operation with the USSR and Bangladesh and is a member of the United Nations and the Commonwealth.
The Constitution: The fundamental rights of all Indian citizens are guaranteed by a written constitution which came into effect in 1950.

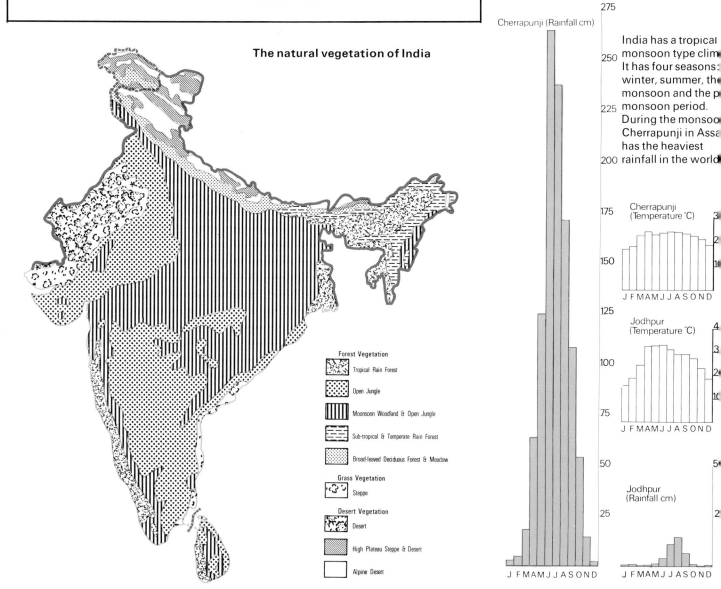

Annual Rainfall cm
300
200
100
50
25

The natural vegetation of India

Forest Vegetation
Tropical Rain Forest
Open Jungle
Moonsoon Woodland & Open Jungle
Sub-tropical & Temperate Rain Forest
Broad-leaved Deciduous Forest & Meadow

Grass Vegetation
Steppe

Desert Vegetation
Desert
High Plateau Steppe & Desert
Alpine Desert

Cherrapunji (Rainfall cm)
275
250
225
200
175
150
125
100
75
50
25
J F M A M J J A S O N D

India has a tropical monsoon type clim It has four seasons: winter, summer, th monsoon and the p monsoon period. During the monsoo Cherrapunji in Assa has the heaviest rainfall in the world

Cherrapunji (Temperature °C)
J F M A M J J A S O N D

Jodhpur (Temperature °C)
J F M A M J J A S O N D

Jodhpur (Rainfall cm)
J F M A M J J A S O N D

The population density

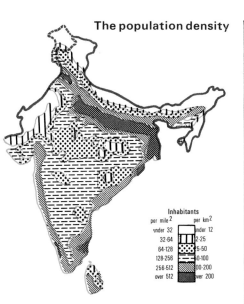

Inhabitants	
per mile^2	per km^2
under 32	under 12
32-64	12-25
64-128	25-50
128-256	50-100
256-512	100-200
over 512	over 200

ndia has one of the fastest growing popu-
ations of the world. Despite government
attempts to encourage family planning, the
opulation rose by about 25 per cent between
961-71. Today it is about 620 million
which makes India the second most
opulous country in the world.

The 1971 census showed that of the
47,949,809 people living in India at that
me, 80 per cent lived in the villages. Delhi
ad the highest population density with
,738 persons per sq. km.

Family planning has not been successful
ecause Indians are very traditional and
elieve in large families. They also benefit
conomically from a large family. Children
elp on the farms and look after their
arents' needs later in life.

Population of principal towns

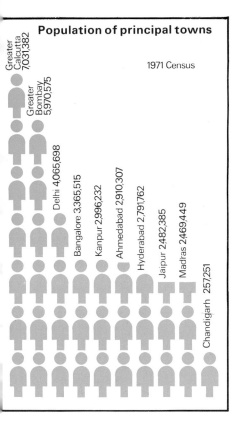

1971 Census

Greater Calcutta 7,031,382
Greater Bombay 5,970,575
Delhi 4,065,698
Bangalore 3,365,515
Kanpur 2,996,232
Ahmedabad 2,910,307
Hyderabad 2,791,762
Jaipur 2482,385
Madras 2469,449
Chandigarh 257,251

Government

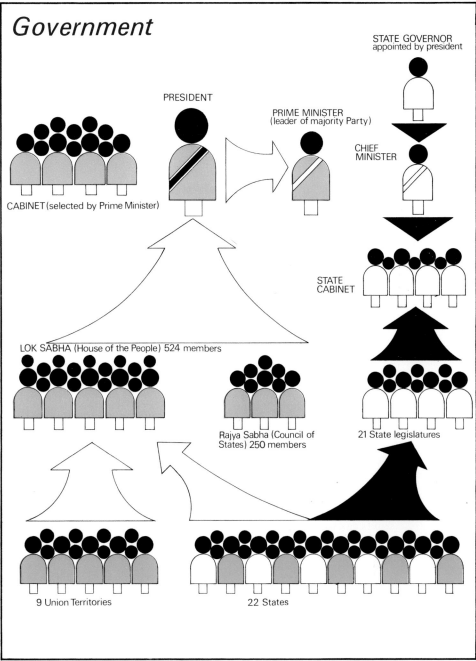

STATE GOVERNOR
appointed by president

PRESIDENT

PRIME MINISTER
(leader of majority Party)

CHIEF MINISTER

CABINET (selected by Prime Minister)

STATE CABINET

LOK SABHA (House of the People) 524 members

Rajya Sabha (Council of States) 250 members

21 State legislatures

9 Union Territories

22 States

The political system of India

India became a sovereign, democratic
republic on January 26th 1950, three years
after it gained independence from British
rule. It has a written constitution.

India has a federal form of govern-
ment. It is a Union of 22 states with
elected State governments and 9
Union territories governed by the
President through administrators. The
Union Government is in Delhi.

Elections are held every five years: in the
States to elect the State Legislatures and
nationally to elect the Lok Sabha, or House
of the People.

Members of the Rajya Sabha, or Council
of States, are elected by the State Legislatures. The President nominates another 12
members. The Council is never dissolved, so
one-third of its members retires every two

years. The Vice-President is the Chairman
of the Council.

The President is the Head of State and is
elected for five years by the Legislatures and
and the two Houses of Parliament. Real
power, however, rests with the Prime
Minister who together with her Cabinet is
responsible to Parliament. Each State has its
own Governor, Chief Minister and State
Cabinet.

The Union Government deals with subjects of all-India importance such as defence
and foreign affairs. The States are responsible
for matters such as law and order, public
health and education. There are 47 subjects
which are dealt with jointly by the States
and the Union.

The Supreme Court, with a Chief Justice
and 13 other Judges appointed by the
President, is the highest court in the land.

55

Reference
History

MAIN EVENTS IN INDIAN HISTORY

NORTH INDIAN HISTORY
B.C.

c. **3000-1500**	The Indus Valley civilization.
c. **1500-500**	Aryans settle along the Ganges. The Vedas are compiled.
c. **599-527**	Mahavira, founder of Jainism.
c. **567-483**	Life of Buddha.
327-326	Alexander invades India.
324	Chandragupta Maurya overthrows the Greeks and founds the first great empire in North India.
273-232	Reign of Ashoka who extends the Mauryan Empire to Mysore.

A.D.

78-144	Kanishka, king of the Kushans rules North and North-west India. Images of Buddha are worshipped.
320	Chandragupta founds the Gupta dynasty in North India.
405-411	Fa Hsien, the Chinese traveller visits the Gupta empire.
455	Hun invasions destroy the Gupta empire.
533	Yasodharman, a central Indian king, defeats the Huns.
606-647	Rule of Harshvardhana. Embassies exchanged with China.
816-1192	Rajput kingdoms in Rajasthan.
1001-1026	Mahmud of Ghazni invades 17 times.
1192	Muhammed of Ghor defeats the Rajputs under Prithviraj Chauhan.
1193	Muhammed's general Qutb-ud-din Aibak takes Delhi.
1206	Qutb-ud-din Aibak founds Slave dynasty.
1290-1526	A succession of Muslim dynasties, the Khiljis, the Tughluqs, the Saiyyads, the Lodis, rule from Delhi.
1398	Timur the Lame invades India.
1469-1538	Guru Nanak, founder of Sikhism.
1526	Babur defeats Ibrahim Lodi and takes Delhi.
1530	Babur dies. Humayun made emperor.
1539-1555	Sher Shah Sur overthrows Humayun and rules from Delhi.
1556	Humayun returns to Delhi and dies.
1556-1605	Reign of Akbar.

1605	Jehangir comes to the throne. Moghul empire covers all India except the Deccan and the extreme South.
1627-1658	Reign of Shah Jehan, the builder of the Taj Mahal.
1630-1680	Life of Shivaji, the Maratha chieftain.
1658-1707	Reign of Aurangzeb.
1664	Shivaji conquers Surat.
1677	Shivaji conquers Carnatic.
1691	Aurangzeb conquers the Deccan.

SOUTH INDIAN HISTORY

30 B.C.-A.D. 543	Satavahanas rule in the Deccan.
	Pandyas rule in Madurai.
436-871	Pallavas rule in Kanchipuram.
	Cheras rule the Malabar coast.
543-753	Chalukyas rule in the Deccan.
753-973	Rashtrakutas seize power from the Chalukyas.
871-1219	Cholas rule from Tanjore.
973-1106	Chalukyas regain the Deccan.
1336-1565	Vijayanagar dynasty rule in the Deccan.
1347-1636	Bahmani dynasty rules Deccan.
1498	Vasco da Gama lands in Calicut.
1510	Portuguese capture Goa.

MODERN INDIAN HISTORY

1600	East India Company granted charter by Queen Elizabeth I.
1611-1615	East India Company builds factories at Surat and Masulipatam.
1639	Madras founded by British.
1668	Bombay given to the Company.
1742	Marathas invade Bengal.
1744-1748	First Anglo-French war. Madras captured by the French and returned after the war.
1757	Battle of Plassey. Clive defeats Siraj-ud-Daulah to regain Calcutta.
1758	Marathas invade the Punjab.
1765	Battle of Buxar. British are granted revenue from Bengal, Bihar and Orissa. Clive made the Governor of Bengal.
1772-1785	Warren Hastings, as Company's Governor-general defeats Hyder Ali in Mysore.
1792	Ranjit Singh, leader of the Sikhs, signs peace treaty with the British.
1798	Wellesley defeats Tipu Sultan.
1819	Marathas finally defeated.
1829-1837	Abolition of *sati* and suppression of *thuggee*.
1843	Conquest of Sind.
1849	Annexation of the Punjab.
1853	Introduction of railways and telegraph system.

1857-1858	The Indian Mutiny.
1858	British India placed under direct government of crown.
1869	Birth of Mahatma Gandhi.
1878	Queen Victoria becomes Empress of India.
1885	Indian National Congress founded.
1905	Partition of Bengal.
1906	Muslim league founded.
1909	Morley-Minto reforms allow for more Indian participation in Government. Separate elections for Muslims introduced.
1912	Capital moved from Calcutta to Delhi.
1914	Gandhi returns to India.
1919	Jallianwalla Bagh massacre.
1920-1922	Non-cooperation movement.
1921	Chamber of Princes formed.
1928	Simon Commission boycotted by Congress.
1930-1935	Civil disobedience.
1930-1932	Round table conferences.
1935	Government of India Act.
1937	Congress returned overwhelmingly in provincial elections.
1939	Congress ministers resign as Britain takes India into World War II without consultation.
1940	Muslim league demand for Pakistan.
1942	Cripps Mission offers Independence after end of war. Rejected by Congress. Quit India movement.
1945-1946	General elections in India. Communal riots in Calcutta and Punjab.
1947	India and Pakistan gain Independence.
1950	India becomes a republic within the Commonwealth.
1952	Jawaharlal Nehru elected India's first Prime Minister.
1961	Goa taken from Portugal.
1962	Sino-Indian border disputes.
1964	Nehru dies. Lal Bahadur Shastri takes over as Prime Minister.
1965	Indo-Pakistan conflict.
1966	Shastri dies in Tashkent during peace talks. Indira Gandhi succeeds as Prime Minister.
1967	Naxalites, a Maoist group in Bengal, seize land to redistribute among peasants.
1971	India at war with Pakistan. Bangladesh becomes Independent.
1974	India explodes nuclear device in Rajasthan desert.
1975	Indira Gandhi accused of electoral malpractice. State of emergency declared.
1977	Congress party defeated in general election. Morarji Desai elected Prime Minister.
1978	Desai visits Britain and USA.
1980	Indira Gandhi re-elected.

NORTH INDIAN RULERS

The Mauryas (324-187 B.C.) Chandragupta Maurya overthrew the Greeks to found Mauryan dynasty. Ashoka was converted to Buddhism and sent missionaries abroad.

The Guptas (320-475 A.D.) Hindu kings whose empire covered North India. Noted for their tolerant rule and patronage of the arts and science. Foreign scholars came to study at Nalanda University. Empire destroyed by Huns.

The Rajputs (c. 600-c. 1600) Descendants of unknown invaders who ruled in Rajasthan. Became Hindus and had a strong code of chivalry. Ruled North India intermittently and presented united opposition to early Arab invaders and Moghuls.

The Delhi Sultanate (1206-1526) Early Muslim rulers of North India. Succession of dynasties beginning with Slave dynasty of Qutb-ud-din Aibak in 1206. Early Muslim rule ended with defeat of Lodi ruler by Babur in 1526.

The Moghuls (1526-1739) Moghul dynasty founded by Babur. Under Akbar, Moghul empire reached its zenith. Noted for its tolerance, he brought Hindu Rajput kings into government and abolished tax on non-Muslims. Restructured the administration and military and introduced fair taxation. The arts flourished. First British traders came to Jahangir's court. Moghul power declined after the reign of Aurangzeb.

RULERS OF THE DECCAN

The Satavahanas (c. 30 B.C.-A.D. 500) Their empire stretched from the Arabian sea to Bay of Bengal. Traded from port near Bombay. Work on Ajanta cave temples started during their rule.

The Chalukyas (550-c.1200) The Chalukyas who ruled from the Godavari valley had a large navy and traded with the Far East. Overthrown by the Rashtrakutas in A.D. 753 but regained power in A.D. 973.

The Vijayanagar Empire (1346-1672) Founded in opposition to rulers of Delhi Sultanate. Capital at Hampi. Home of Hindu culture during 16th century.

The Marathas (1630-1819) The Marathas rose under Shivaji to fight against the Moghul emperor Aurangzeb. After Shivaji's death the Marathas split into many kingdoms but they united to capture Delhi. Fought off Afghan invasions and raided South India, Bengal and the Punjab. Defeated by British in 1819.

SOUTH INDIAN RULERS

Earliest known South Indian dynasties were Pandyas of Madurai, Cheras of Malabar coast and Cholas of Tanjore.

The Pallavas (436-871) Ruled from Kanchipuram. Had good navy and army. Fought against Chalukyas in the Deccan.

The Cholas (871-1279) Defeated Pallavas. Capital at Tanjore. Had large navy and traded with Far East. Built canals and temples.

The Arts

GREAT PERIODS OF INDIAN ART

Buddhist period (250 B.C.-A.D. 300) Ashoka's highly-polished stone pillars topped with animals and flowers. The stupas with ornately carved stone gateways. Ajanta cave temples hewn out of rock and decorated with frescoes and religious sculpture. The Greek-influenced Gandhara school of sculpture flourished under the Kushans. Images of Buddha were made, which resemble Greek gods. At Mathura, Indian style developed in red stone with voluptuous *yakshis*, superhuman women.

Early Hindu period (300-600) Under Gupta rule the arts flourished. Gupta mathematicians used decimals and algebra in their calculations. Astronomers knew the Earth is round and rotates on its axis.

Later Hindu period (600-1200) Two different styles of architecture in North and South India. North Indian temples were somewhat pineapple-shaped. South Indian temples made use of pillars and were built like pyramids. Examples of South Indian or Dravidian style are the Pallava rock cut temples at Mahabalipuram made to look like chariots. The huge pyramid of the Shiva temple at Tanjore. The Madurai temples with their long pillared halls and imposing gateways covered with sculpture. In the Deccan the Rashtrakuta rock cut temples of Ellora and Elephanta were influenced by Dravidian ideas. North Indian architecture is best seen at Khajuraho, Konarak, Bhubaneshvar and Rajasthan. Most important sculpture of South India are the Chola bronze statues, made by the lost wax method. Painting on palm leaves by Jains in Gujarat and under Pala rulers in Bengal.

Moghul period (1500-1700) Muslim architects gave India the dome, the spire, and the arch. Akbar built his capital in red sandstone at Fatehpur Sikri. Best examples of Moghul architecture are the Taj Mahal, the Red Fort and the Jumma Masjid in Delhi. Important schools of miniature painting are the Moghul school, the Rajput schools such as Mewar, Kishangarh, and Hill schools of Kangra and Basholi.

British Raj (1857-1947) Victorian gothic architecture in Bombay and Calcutta. Bengali school of painting under Abhanindranath Tagore. Other Indian painters of the time: Rabindranath Tagore, Jamini Roy and Amrita Sher-gil.

Modern period Ultra-modern city of Chandigarh built by Le Corbusier. Modern Indian painters such as Satish Gujral and Hussain influenced by Indian folk art and by European art. Drama in Indian languages becoming popular. Indian film directors such as Satyajit Ray and Mrinal Sen making films on social themes.

PHILOSOPHERS AND THINKERS

Buddha (c. 567-483 B.C.) Founder of Buddhism. Preached that the only way to overcome suffering was to attain *Nirvana*, ultimate bliss.

Mahavira (c. 540-467 B.C.) Founder of Jainism, a strict non-violent religion. He believed the universe is eternal and everything has a soul.

Kautilya (321-296 B.C.) Chief minister to Chandragupta Maurya. Wrote the *Arthashastra* on the art of government.

Patanjali (c. 300 B.C.) Wrote the *Yoga Sutra* on the philosophy and practise of yoga.

Shankaracharya (788-820 A.D.) Preached that man's soul and God were one. He reinterpreted the Vedas.

Ramanuja (12th century A.D.) He preached a simpler form of Hinduism without ritual, just *Bhakti* or pure devotion to God.

Guru Nanak (1469-1538) Founder of Sikhism.

Raja Ram Mohan Roy (1780-1833) Hindu reformer and founder of sect called the Brahmo Samaj. Against idol worship and ritual. Helped to abolish child marriage and *sati*.

Mohandas Karamchand Gandhi (1869-1948) Developed non-violence into a way of life and used it to achieve political ends. His autobiography is called *The Story of my Experiments with Truth*.

LITERATURE

The Vedas (Sanskrit c. 1500 B.C.-c. 500 B.C.) Hindu scriptures divided into 4 books; *Rig Veda, Sama Veda, Yajur Veda* and *Atharva Veda*. They contain hymns, descriptions of rituals and sacrifices, and philosophical discussions.

Vyasa (Sanskrit c. 900-500 B.C.) Wrote epic poem *Mahabharata*. The *Bhagavad Gita*, part of the *Mahabharata*, encapsulates Hindu philosophy.

Valmiki (Sanskrit c. 500 B.C.) Author of the *Ramayana*, a long epic poem about the life of the god Rama.

The Tipitaka (Pali 477 B.C.) Buddhist scriptures containing Buddha's sermons and the *Jatakas*, Buddhist stories.

Ilango Adigal (Tamil c. 200 B.C.-A.D. 100) Wrote *Shilappadikaram*, an epic about the trials of a Tamil couple as they travel through the South Indian kingdoms.

Kalidasa (Sanskrit c. 400 A.D.) Poet and dramatist of the Gupta period, wrote the *Cloud Messenger* and *Shakuntala*.

Jayadeva (Sanskrit 1200) Wrote *Gita Govinda*, songs in praise of the god Krishna.

Tulsidas (Hindi 1532-1623) Rewrote the *Ramayana* in Hindi as *Ramacharitamanas*.

Ghalib (Urdu and Persian) His work is the best example of the flowering of Urdu poetry in the 19th century. Wrote *Diwan-e-Ghalib*.

Rabindranath Tagore (Bengali 1861-1941) Won the Nobel prize for *Gitanjali*, song offerings, and author of Indian National anthem.

R. K. Narayan One of many modern Indian writers in English. His novels include *The Maneater of Malgudi* and *The Guide*.

Reference
The Economy

FACTS AND FIGURES

Total wealth produced: (1972-3)
Rs. 385,730 million (about
£21,430 million).

Main trading partners: United
Kingdom, United States, Canada,
Japan, Soviet Union and Eastern
European countries.

Main sources of income:
Agriculture: Wheat, rice, maize,
barley and other cereals, pulses,
coconuts, spices, tea, cotton, silk,
jute, timber.
Mining: Iron and steel, coal, some
oil and natural gas, manganese, mica,
bauxite and precious stones. India has
vast mineral resources which still
remain to be exploited.
Industry: Heavy electrical and non-
electrical machinery, agricultural and
electronic equipment, machine tools,
textiles, chemicals and
pharmaceuticals.
Others: Handicrafts, hides,
fertilizers, fish and shellfish.

Currency: The unit of currency is
the rupee (Rs.) which is divided into
100 naya paisas, since
decimalization in 1957. The official
rate of exchange (1978) is
£1 = Rs. 18.

Agriculture in India

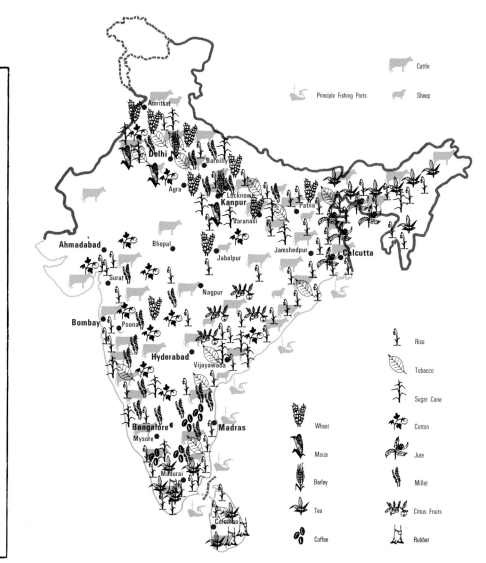

Imports and exports

Indian exports have undergone a remarkable
change since 1947. Under British rule, they
were restricted to a few agriculture-based
products and some minerals. Today India
exports nearly 3,000 different products to
almost every country in the world. These
include railway wagons, transmission line
towers, chemical plants and electronic
equipment.

India leads the world in the production of
feature films. These are exported to the
Middle East, Africa, the Far East, the Soviet
Union and countries which have large Indian
immigrant populations. In spite of this, India
imports more than it exports. It needs
sophisticated machinery, scarce raw materials
and oil for its developing industries.

When the monsoon fails, India has to
import vast quantities of wheat to feed its
people. The new strains of wheat which give
better yields are expensive and require
special chemical fertilizers which can only be
bought from abroad.

As India develops agriculturally, it will
become self-sufficient in food and so improve
its trade balance.

What is imported and exported (1975-76)
Economic Survey 1976-77

(figures in million Rs)

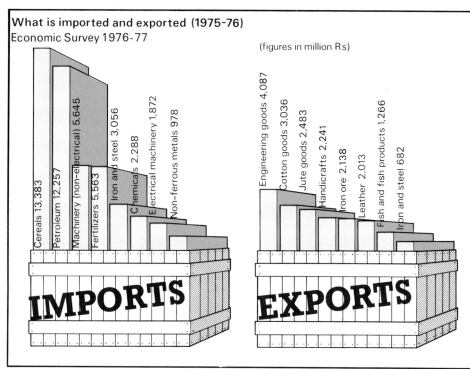

IMPORTS

Cereals 13,383
Petroleum 12,257
Machinery (non-electrical) 5,645
Fertilizers 5,563
Iron and steel 3,056
Chemicals 2,288
Electrical machinery 1,872
Non-ferrous metals 978

EXPORTS

Engineering goods 4,087
Cotton goods 3,036
Jute goods 2,483
Handicrafts 2,241
Iron ore 2,138
Leather 2,013
Fish and fish products 1,266
Iron and steel 682

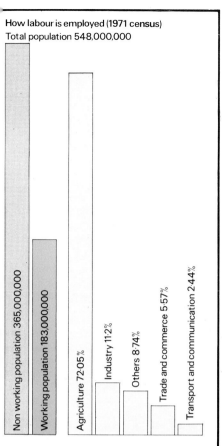

How labour is employed (1971 census)
Total population 548,000,000

- Non working population 365,000,000
- Working population 183,000,000
- Agriculture 72·05%
- Industry 11·2%
- Others 8·74%
- Trade and commerce 5·57%
- Transport and communication 2·44%

India is an agricultural society. Over 70 per cent of its people work on the land to produce 44 per cent of the country's wealth.
Unemployment is very high because of the rising population and the slow growth of industry. Many Indians go to work in other countries.

Industry in India

Principal Coalmining Areas
Oilfields
Oil Refineries
Lignite
Iron metallurgy
Chemicals
Textiles

Cement
Paper & Pulp
Tobacco Manufacturing
Sugar Refineries
Pottery
Glass
Shoes
Leather

Major Industrial Centres
Mechanical Engineering
Shipbuilding
Aeroplanes
Motor Vehicles
Bicycles

...ve-year plans

...hen India gained Independence in 1947, ...agricultural and mineral resources were ...inly unexploited. It was decided to ...velop them in a series of five-year plans.
...The first started in 1951 and was a great ...ccess. It concentrated on agriculture, ...gation and hydro-electric power. Some ...India's biggest dams were built during ...s period.
...The second five-year plan gave highest ...ority to the development of industry. ...ree new steel works were built and ...undations were laid for heavy engineering ...d mechanical industries. Cement and ...per factories were started for the first time ...d fertilizer plants were expanded.
...India's third plan suffered because of ...nflicts with China and Pakistan. Foreign ...l was cut off, industry ran short of raw ...terials and the monsoons failed. The ...urth plan also fell short of its targets.
...The fifth five-year plan was terminated in ...77 by the Janata party. The sixth five-...ar plan (1980-1985) aims to develop ...e oil industry and improve transport ...d delivery.

How India's economy improved 1950-71

	1950/1	1970/1
Rice (cleaned) '000 tonnes	20,576	42,735
Wheat '000 tonnes	6,462	26,477
Electricity Kwh	5,300 million	55,800 million
Irrigated areas hectares	22.6 million	37.2 million 1969/70
Coal '000 tonnes	32,800	74,300
Iron ore '000 tonnes	3,000	22,500
Steel and finished steel '000 tonnes	2,510	10,620
Nitrogenous fertilizers '000 tonnes	9	830
Phosphatic fertilizers '000 tonnes	9	229
Petroleum products (refined) '000 tonnes	200	17,100
Jute textiles '000 tonnes	837	958
Cotton cloth metres	4,215	7,596

Gazetteer

Agra (27 09N 78 00E) Site of the Taj Mahal. Large handicrafts industry and tourist trade.

Ahmedabad (23 03N 74 40E) Houses an Indian space research centre and is surrounded by cotton mills. Site of the famous Jumma Masjid.

Allahabad (25 57N 81 50E) The "City of God" at the junction of the rivers Ganges and Jumna. A place of pilgrimage for the Hindus during the Kumbh Mela held every 12 years. Famous university town.

Amritsar (31 35N 74 56E) Manufacturing city. Site of the famous Golden Temple built by the Sikh Guru Ram Das. Contains the Granth Sahib, the sacred book of the Sikhs.

Andaman and Nicobar Islands 223 islands in the Bay of Bengal. Formerly used as a British penal colony.

Assam Chief tea growing state of India with 750 plantations. Rich in minerals including oil and natural gas. Two refineries in operation.

Bangalore (12 58N 77 35E) Capital of Karnataka. Light engineering industry and aircraft factory. Headquarters of the Indian Institute of Science.

Bhubaneswar Capital of Orissa. Has some beautiful Hindu temples dating from the 8th to 10th century, the most famous being the Lingaraj temple.

Bihar Major industrial state. Contains Tata steel mills, locomotive factories in Jamshedpur and the Sindri fertilizer plant built in 1952.

Bombay (18 56N 72 51E) Built on seven islets, its harbour is the ocean gateway to Western India. Surrounded by refineries and nuclear research laboratories and reactors in Trombay. Capital of Maharashtra.

Brahmaputra The main river of E. India. Its 1,800 miles (2,897 km) pass through Tibet, Assam, Bengal and Bangladesh. Means "son of Brahma".

Calcutta (22 35N 88 21E) Capital of West Bengal, built on the banks of the Hooghly river. Main export harbour for India's tea and jute trade. Has many refugees from Bangladesh.

Cape Comorin (8 04N 77 35E) Southernmost tip of the Indian peninsula. Also called Kanniyakumari.

Chandigarh (30 43N 76 47E) The capital of Haryana and the Punjab. Designed by the French architect Le Corbusier.

Cochin (9 56N 76 15E) Large shipyard under construction. Natural harbour used for sea trade in coconuts and tea.

Deccan Plateau south of the Vindhya mountains. Cotton growing area.

Delhi (28 40N 77 14E) The capital of India, strategically placed to guard the rich Indo-Gangetic plain. Site of the Moghul Red Fort, Qutb Minar, the famous sandstone monument and several other historic buildings. New Delhi was designed by Sir Edward Lutyens.

Fatehpur Sikri (27 06N 77 39E) Ancient Moghul capital of India. Built in red sandstone, its remains include palaces, audience halls, tombs and the great gate of victory, the Buland Darwaza.

Ganges The sacred river of India, also called Ganga. Rises in the Himalayas on India's northeast border. Flows S.E. through Uttar Pradesh, Bihar and Bengal to merge with the Brahmaputra in the delta basin leading to the Bay of Bengal. Sacred cities of the Hindus lie on its banks.

Ghats, Eastern and Western Two forested mountain ranges bounding the Deccan peninsula. Main source of India's timber. The W. Ghats average 4,000 ft. (1,219m) and the E. Ghats 2,000 ft. (610m) in height.

Goa Originally a Portuguese settlement, made part of India in 1961. There is a strong Portuguese influence in the language, architecture and food.

Gujarat W. Indian state with oil and gas reserves in Ankleshwar, Cambay and Calol.

Himalayas In Sanskrit "the abode of snow". Gigantic northern wall of India from Assam in the East to Kashmir in the West. Contains some of the world's highest peaks. Only the southern ranges are in India.

Hyderabad (17 22N 78 26E) Capital of Andhra Pradesh. Contains the Char Minar and several other mosques as well as the Nizam's palace. From the 17th century onwards, the rulers of Hyderabad controlled most of the N. Deccan. Surrounded by tobacco and fruit orchards.

Indus River flowing from the Tibetan Himalayas, through Sind and Punjab into the Arabian sea. The five rivers of the Punjab all flow into its 1,700 mile (2,736 km) length.

Jaipur (26 53N 75 50E) The capital of Rajasthan. An important commercial centre. It has beautiful palaces, gardens and parks built by the Maharajahs.

Jammu (32 43N 74 54E) Winter capital of state of Jammu and Kashmir. Research centre for medicine.

Jammu and Kashmir Mountainous N.W. state of India with many beautiful river valleys. A fertile agricultural state and a popular tourist centre with winter skiing. Scene of disputes between India and Pakistan.

Jumna (Yamuna) One of the 12 sacred rivers of the Hindus. Flows from the Himalayas for 860 miles (1,384 km) to the Ganges at Allahabad. Historically an important trade highway.

Kerala S.W. Indian state bordering on the Arabian sea. First state in India to elect democratically a Communist government. Kerala has the highest literacy rate in India.

Karnataka (formerly known as Myso Occupies the plateau region of the S. Dec A prosperous state, watered by tributarie the Kistna and Cauvery rivers. Contains fields.

Lakshadweep Group of 15 coral isla 200 miles W. of Madras. Formerly know the Laccadive, Minicoy and Amindivi Isla

Lucknow (26 50N 80 54E) Capital of U Pradesh. Manufacturing town with rail workshops built on the banks of the Go The centre of Indian Muslim culture, it c tains the Imambara mausoleum of Asa Daula. The relief of Lucknow was one of most dramatic episodes of the Indian Mu

Madras (13 05N 80 18E) Capital of T. Nadu. Main commercial centre of S.E. I and trading port. Centre of South Inc film industry.

Madhya Pradesh An agricultural and m ing state in Central India. Contains the c newsprint mill at Nepa Nagar, the B steel mills and beautiful national parks game reserves.

Nagpur (21 01n 79 12E) Until rece the capital of Madhya Pradesh. important town and railway junct with an imposing fort and univers

Nagaland This state on the N.E. bo between India and Burma houses the fier independent Naga hill tribes.

Orissa This E. Indian maritime state developed large mineral-based indust since 1947. There are steel and ferti plants at Rourkela, as well as sugar, a and chemical plants. Iron ore is mined b for Indian use and for export to Japan.

Patna (23 57N 85 12E) The capital of B is an ancient city and place of pilgrima Built on the banks of the Ganges, it was f long time the centre of opium manufactur It is now well-known for rice growing.

Pondicherry Union territory. Was a for French settlement which transferred Indian rule in 1954.

Poona (18 34N 73 58E) Bombay's hill sort and former British military centre.

Punjab The "land of the five rivers" is ca the "granary" of India. After the Mog Empire collapsed, the Sikhs became one the dominant powers.

Rajasthan Largely desert state in N India, mined for lead, zinc and preci stones. India exploded her first nucl device here in the desert.

Simla (31 07N 77 09E) Capital of Himac Pradesh. Under British rule it was the su mer residence of the Viceroy, and the cer of British social life.

Trivandrum Capital of Kerala in S. India seaport with temples, a palace and zoo.

Varanasi (25 20N 83 00E) formerly kno as Benares. The most sacred city of Hindus, on the banks of the Ganges, c tains numerous temples. Cremations are p formed in the burning ghats, while pilgr bathe in the sacred waters at other ghats.

Visakhatapatam (17 42N 83 42E) M seaport of Andhra Pradesh, on the Bay Bengal. It has a harbour, a large refinery a ship-building industry.

ndex